MEET
JEREMIAH

MEET JEREMIAH

A Devotional Commentary

BURTON L. GODDARD

KREGEL PUBLICATIONS
Grand Rapids, Michigan 49501

Cover Photo: Art Jacobs
Cover and Book Design: Al Hartman

Library of Congress Cataloging-in Publication Data
Goddard, Burton L.
   Meet Jeremiah: meditations on his words / Burton L. Goddard.
     p.   cm.
   1. Bible. O.T. Jeremiah—Meditations. I. Title.
BS1525.4.G635   1991   224'.206—dc20   91-21205
                                            CIP

ISBN 0-8254-2728-2

     1 2 3 4 5 Printing/Year 95 94 93 92

Printed in the United States of America

Contents

Preface

These meditations, first published in *The Presbyterian Guardian*, are reprinted by permission. The original text has been revised slightly. Scripture references from the *New International Version* have replaced those from the *King James Version*.

Dr. Goddard contributed several series of meditations to the *Guardian*, concerning which the managing editor, Thomas R. Birch, commented at various times. Speaking of the editorial council he said, "It was unanimously the opinion of the members that your devotionals were the best that they had ever read." On another occasion he wrote: "Letter after letter comes to me in praise of your work . . . . Just as an example of this I quote a paragraph from a letter received this morning . . . . 'Mr. Goddard's exquisite style and earnestness of expression put him on a par with the best.'"

At the time, the author's busy schedule as Dean of Gordon College and Gordon Divinity School precluded his readying the meditations for publication in book form. In retirement, however, he decided to prepare the devotionals for a wider audience.

It is his hope that the book will give the reader a broad grasp of what the Book of Jeremiah is all about, together with a feeling that he or she really knows the great prophet. More than that, the author desires that readers' hearts will be searched in the light of the Word so that they will be brought face to face with the importance of a right relationship with God and a daily walk pleasing to Him.

1

Commissioned a Prophet

JEREMIAH 1:1-9

I was quite young when I first met him. He seemed like a veiled figure. I knew little about him. I suppose that was the reason. Now it is all different. I feel a sympathetic interest in the ups and downs of his life. My own heart has experienced somewhat of the conflict, the longing, the call of duty that was his. I admire him. I can almost say that I love him. Of whom do I speak? Jeremiah, the prophet.

The Call

Perhaps the other boys with whom he played as a lad envied him. His father was a priest. The dark shadow of uncertainty clouds his boyhood in the little town of Anathoth, a few miles to the north of Jerusalem, but no great stretch of the imagination is necessary to follow the boy Jeremiah on an early visit to the temple city. His youthful mind is active. He marvels at the splendor of the great sanctuary. Fascinated by a thousand details of the ritual of sacrifice, he watches the priests at work—notes the uniqueness of their dress. At home again, he plies his father with questions. What does it all mean? And if we may conceive of a priest, awakened to the sacredness of his calling and treasuring faith in his bosom as a result of the spiritual awakening of his king, the godly Josiah, we may well imagine that young Jeremiah was well indoctrinated and came to know the covenant God of his fathers.

And so, when God one day revealed Himself to him and called him to service, the Revealing One did not come as a stranger. In Jeremiah's Damascus Road experience he did not need to cry out, "Who are You, Lord?" There was no agnostic question in his heart. He knew in whom he had believed. He believed more truly than thousands in Judah, for he knew God as the great sovereign of *all* nature and *all* the kingdoms of men. He did not doubt the unlimited power of the Most High. He was a *prepared* vessel, evidencing the certain predestination and careful providence of the all-wise God.

To such a man, still at a tender age, with the prospect of long years of service, God spoke:

> *Before I formed you in the womb I knew you,*
> *before you were born I set you apart;*
> *I appointed you as a prophet to the nations.*

Have words of Scripture ever burned themselves deep into your conscience, penetrating "even to dividing soul and spirit"? Have the thoughts and intents of your heart ever been swiftly divided to make way for the voice of the Lord— "My son, give me your heart"— "Come to me"—"Turn, turn . . . . Why will you die?"—"Go and make disciples"—? Then, like Jeremiah, you have heard a call from God. Then you have experienced the awe-inspiring solemnity of listening to the voice of the almighty God.

Hesitation

Jeremiah knew that the call was right and just and good. His regenerated nature thrilled at the prospect of prophesying for his God. Perhaps his imagination envisaged the time when he might stand before kings to declare the counsel of the Lord with the awful words, "This is what the Lord says."

Jeremiah also knew, however, the fate that too often had come to the prophets of God. Like his Messiah to come, he knew that the prophets had been killed. Like the writer of Hebrews, he thought of the cruel mockings and scourgings that came to those sent by God. No doubt he thought of the ill treatment accorded Amos at Bethel, of the child voices raised in insult against the bald prophet, Elisha, and of Jezebel's wrath toward Elijah.

Unfailing faith and firm courage would be required of a prophet. His natural timidity would have to be overruled. He would have to lay bare the sore spots of sin in people's lives. Not concerned to spare feelings, he would have to declare righteous judgment on the land he loved. It was no light task to which his Lord summoned him.

The old nature asserted itself. In the weakness of uncertainty and indecision he answered,

> *Ah, Sovereign Lord, I do not know how to speak; I am only a child.*

What Christian has not experienced such conflict? The mighty Paul, who delighted in the law of God after the inward man, was aware of another law in his members warring against his regenerate nature. On occasion *you* may have known the acceptable way and may have hesitated while considering what you told yourself was your own best reasoning but what was in reality the voice of the Tempter. Would you rebuke Jeremiah? "At whatever point you judge the other, you are condemning yourself" (Rom. 2:1). May God have mercy on you as He did on Jeremiah!

Assurance

God knows our weakness. He knew that of Jeremiah. Tenderly, firmly, He answered:

> *Do not say, "I am only a child." You must go to everyone I send you to and say whatever I command you. Do not be afraid of them, for I am with you and will rescue you.*

There could be no objection in the face of such assurance. The murmur died from the young man's lips. His hesitation disappeared. If God be for him, who could be against him? If the pillar of cloud and of fire should guide his way, he did not need to fear. Was not this the song of Jeremiah?

> When through fiery trials thy pathway shall lie,
>   My grace, all sufficient, shall be thy supply;
> The flame shall not hurt thee; I only design
>   Thy dross to consume, and thy gold to refine.

With some such song in his heart, Jeremiah went on, faith kindled anew in his breast. But this was not all. An unforgettable drama ensued. We turn to his own statement:

> *Then the Lord reached out his hand and touched my mouth and said to me, "Now, I have put my words in your mouth. See, today I appoint you over nations and kingdoms to uproot and tear down, to destroy and overthrow, to build and to plant."*

The divine call was divinely sealed. Hereafter Jeremiah would speak not only his own wisdom but the pure word of the Lord. God had commissioned him to be a prophet of prophets.

Your call may not be so noteworthy. You may not stand before kings. You will not be a like vehicle of inspired revelation. But God has called or will call each of His elect to a chosen post in Kingdom service. Before you came from the womb, He sanctified you and ordained you for a particular office.

The path of service to which God calls may be difficult, filled with hazards and beset with dangers, but God will be with you, your refuge and fortress. You no longer live, but Christ lives in you, and you can do all things in His strength. Do not say, "I am only a child."

2

The Task of a Prophet

JEREMIAH 1:10

I t is the night of election day. As the returns are tabulated it soon becomes apparent that one of the candidates has been victorious. He has thrown himself unreservedly into the campaign. Now he is exultant, proud. He thinks only of the glory of his victory. It is not long, however, until the flush of excitement dies away. He is called upon to face soberly the tasks of his new office. He finds that he has a multitude of duties and responsibilities. Many of them are hard; some are unpleasant. He shrinks from the performance of the most objectionable ones. He wishes it might be otherwise.

Sweeping Destruction

Jeremiah must have experienced similar feelings in his day. There was glory in being a prophet of the living God, but the prophetic task was most exacting. The words of God's commission were almost stern, less sweet than bitter, staggering in their import:

> *See, today I appoint you over nations and kingdoms to uproot and tear down, to destroy and overthrow.*

Doubtless Jeremiah had the optimistic vision of youth. There was nothing of the cynic in his makeup. How he would have loved to preach God's covenant faithfulness, His great mercy, His loving-kindness, the coming of His Kingdom of peace! If only his message could be a positive one!

But alas! Was it true? Had he heard correctly? Must he indeed "uproot," "tear down," "destroy," "overthrow"? Must denunciation have the first and great place in his ministry? How he loathed the thought! How he inwardly rebelled against it!

It is not easy for a minister of Jesus Christ to preach a message contrary to the popular current of the times in which he lives. He shrinks from the duty of exposing and denouncing the specific sins that are ruining the lives of the people about him. He finds it hard to fight against the pleasures that are keeping his flock from usefulness in Christ's service. Yet his prophetic calling demands that he do so.

There has probably never been a time when it was otherwise. Noah's ministry was one of condemnation. Enoch lashed out against the ungodliness of his age. Moses pronounced God's judgment against his people and led them year after year, knowing that he could never take them into the Promised Land. Amos found it necessary to disillusion Israel and make it clear to her people that the great Day of the Lord would bring them not salvation but destruction. The apostle Paul learned how impossible it was to please both men and God. Jeremiah was called upon to sound the death knell of the kingdom of Judah, to rebuke a nation for its idolatry, and to pronounce divine sentence against a rebellious people.

Nor is the negative task of the minister without reason. God's kingdom cannot be planted in a heart as long as Satan holds the throne of that heart. A "stony heart" must be replaced by "a heart of flesh." Old cars may be reconditioned and made relatively good; old houses may be renovated and repainted to rival the appearance of new ones; but the unregenerate nature of man must be utterly destroyed if he is to enter the kingdom of heaven. And the idols of a nation must be broken and burned if that nation is to be acceptable before God.

I am greatly concerned when a minister of Christ has no enemies. It was not so in the days of Jeremiah and the prophets of old. It was not so in the days of the earthly ministry of the Son of God. It was not so in the days of Paul and Athanasius, Luther and Calvin, Whitefield and Edwards. Sin must be met and defeated on the battlefield of people's hearts, for people themselves are content to live and die in their sins.

It is only the divine Word brought by God's faithful prophets, a mighty hammer of the Holy Spirit, that will be successful in battering away the defenses of the Evil One and making way for the entrance of eternal life. It was a faithful minister who said, "There are many in my community who love me; the rest hate me." He was hated because, like the noble Lincoln, when he had opportunity to hit sin, he hit it hard.

Constructive Upbuilding

It is highly questionable, however, whether any one called to prophetic duty is ever given a ministry solely of condemnation. There have always been those who occupy themselves in work of destruction and who have no constructive program, no new foundation to lay, no blueprints for another structure, no energy to supply a new framework, no resources, no vision, no desire. The world despises such people. God has no use for them.

The Lord was not content that Jeremiah should be of that stripe. He must rebuke people for their sin, but he must also preach the gospel of salvation. He must show the temporary character of the old covenant; he must paint the glories of the new. He must declare the fate of a sinful kingdom; he must herald God's promises to a faithful remnant. The commission of his God would not only have him to root out and destroy, but also "to build and to plant."

There is something wrong with a pastor who does not "build" and "plant." There is something wrong with a Christian who criticizes and condemns but who fails to live and speak the good news of salvation and forgiveness. There is something wrong with the church that has no positive message and program but is free in its attack upon various sects and individuals. The wrong lies in the fact that it has undertaken *only part* of the task of the prophet. And *only part*, whichever part it may be, is utterly wrong in the sight of God.

The one-sidedness of the teachers of the law and the Pharisees was denounced by Christ when He said, "You should have practiced the latter without leaving the former undone" (Luke 11:42).

You know where the neglect lies if you have failed to shoulder the *twofold* task of a prophet. You know where your church has failed. But there is forgiveness with God. Ask—and receive. Confess your failure. Then start anew to do the *full* work of a prophet.

3

Living Water and Broken Cisterns

JEREMIAH 2:13

C hip! Chip! Chip! It is the sound of a chisel working against stubborn stone. A man is stooped at his task. The chisel slips. He swears. He works more intensely, for he is nearing the completion of his project. At times his strength almost fails. It has been an arduous task.

Evil thoughts possess his mind. He is cutting a cistern into the rock. There he will store the sweet waters of the earth. Folks call him crazy because he persists in the task while a crystal streamlet of mountain water sparkles and leaps the year round over the stones of the stream bed adjacent to his little mountain cabin. But, he muses, he is not crazy. He is only proud, too proud to dip his pail into the pure water God sends coursing so freely down the mountain. He wants nothing to do with God. He will accept no favors at His hand. He can get along very well without God, thank you!

The last stroke sounds. The work is done. Now dark clouds blot out the sun, and sheets of rain break against the bare rocks. An exultant glee possesses the worker. His triumph will soon be demonstrated.

An Empty Cistern

Hours of darkness allow time for the fallen drops to seep through the topsoil to rock layers below. The cistern digger approaches. He laughs an unholy laugh as he fastens a rope to the bucket and dangles it at the mouth of the cistern. Anticipating a noisy splash, he casts the bucket from him. He waits but a moment. Then to his ears comes a harsh, metallic sound. It echoes upward, reverberating again and again. The echoes die. The awful truth is apparent. The cistern is empty! Dry! Perhaps the God of Creation, aware from all eternity of this blasphemous undertaking, had long ago sent an earthquake to loosen the rocks and make them incapable of holding heaven's waters.

Disappointment, rage, despair, hatred and bitterness strive against one another for mastery of the man's mind. No one of them is really successful. He curses God, shakes his fist as though to brandish it in the face of the Almighty, beats his breast, and then, stark mad, leaps to his death in the broken cistern he has carved out with his own hands. "Bloody and deceitful men dig their own graves."

Beside the cabin, God's fresh streamlet plays quietly on its way, and thirsty adventurers stoop to drink, quaff pure draughts, and continue their journey refreshed.

Is this merely the parable of men whose minds have failed and whose insane acts are excusable? Would to God it were, but it is not. It stands for an ungrateful people who had turned every one to their own way and had forsaken their covenant God. It represents a proud nation, gone away into idolatry, entirely unrepentant. The word of the Lord came to Jeremiah, saying,

> *My people have committed two sins:*
> *They have forsaken me,*
>   *the spring of living water,*
> *and have dug their own cisterns,*
>   *broken cisterns that cannot hold water.*

The Lord God had been the only hope of Israel. He had redeemed them from Egypt. He had led them through the wilderness.
He had brought them into the Land of Promise.

At first their love for Him had been warm and constant. Then sin
had wooed them away. Their pride constrained them to demand an
earthly king that they might be like the nations. The theocratic rule
of their God did not satisfy their vanity.

Lessons from History

But their first king was rejected by God and later took his own
life. Large numbers joined in rebellion to unseat his successor. The
third king taxed the people so heavily that the kingdom split in two
at his death. Later kings were often weak, inefficient, bloodthirsty,
cruel, and helpless before invading princes. Yet Israel refused to
confess her sin and return to the God of her fathers, a King of
unrestrained power who had ruled them with unmeasured mercy
and love. She had seemingly preferred broken cisterns to the Fountain of Living Water.

Times had gone from bad to worse. The very existence of the
nation had been threatened. Would not the weary people now call
on their God of old? The prophets urged them to do so. Stubborn
and proud, they refused. Rather, they turned to the rising star of the
East, Great Assyria, and prostrated themselves to entreat mercy of
her. Now, in the time of Jeremiah, they had repudiated their former
alliance and were courting favor with neighbors who worshiped the
sun. The parable suits the situation. They heard the prophetic voice,
"Come, all you who are thirsty, come to the waters" (Isa. 55:1)—but
they kept on building broken cisterns.

The day of testing was sure to come. It did. All their cisterns were
dry. Soldiers from the East razed the temple, carried away its vessels of silver and gold, and left the kingdom desolate. The flower of
the land faded. Night descended. Israel would have done well to
turn to the Fountain of Living Water.

History Repeats Itself

I know of another people who have not profited by Israel's
example. I know of a people who have forsaken their God. *It is the*

people among whom we live. Their fathers would not live without availing themselves of the water of life offered freely to all by the Divine Son, our Savior. This people is content to hew out cisterns of wealth and fame, of success and valor. But in the day when God will judge men and nations, those cisterns will be found to have run dry.

Even before the Day of Judgment, the dryness of such cisterns may become apparent. All our nation's defenses may be found to be insecure. As the heavy hand of judgment fell on ancient Israel, so may that same hand fall on the nation we love. O that our people might turn to the One who offers "living water"—turn before it is too late!

Let us not be mistaken. We do but hew out broken cisterns. They may hold enough brackish water to tide us over temporary crises, but unless we turn to the Great Fountain, they will send us out into eternity with parched, lost souls.

I have been commissioned by Jeremiah's God to bid my countrymen to hearken to the gracious words of God's own Son: "Whoever drinks the water I give him will never thirst. Indeed, the water I give him will become in him a spring of water welling up to eternal life" (John 4:14).

Let everyone put his pride away, cast his chisel from him, humble himself at the foot of the cross. By faith, let him lay hold on the gospel offer of life eternal. Let him turn forever from the broken cisterns of earth, and let him come, "take the free gift of the water of life" (Rev. 22:17).

4

Heart Washing
JEREMIAH 2:22; 4:14

I n the fourth chapter of his prophecy, Jeremiah calls to mind the vivid imagery of the hot east wind of Palestine as it sweeps in scorching blasts across the hills. Its fierce gusts are almost incessant. There is grain to be winnowed, but not with such a wind. The gale would carry away both wheat and chaff. It is a destructive force. Men fear its approach.

The figure is that of impending judgment upon the city of Jerusalem and the people of the Southern Kingdom. A dread enemy is to sweep upon her like a mighty whirlwind. It is as though the chariots of war are already bearing down on them, as though the sun strikes thousands of helmets and leaps from them in tongues of golden fire. The voice of Jerusalem is loud with cries of woe. Hope has perished from the hearts of her inhabitants. In confusion and fear they wait hopelessly for the blow to fall.

Just at this moment a message comes to the despairing populace.

In deep, measured tones it commands audience. It is the voice of the God they have forsaken. It is stern because of its demands, yet it is truly a voice of love and grace, of mercy and hope:

O Jerusalem, wash the evil from your heart and be saved.

The one hope of Israel in that darkest hour of her existence lay in the washing of her heart from sin. There was no other way by which she could be saved. Yes, God has no other way of salvation, whether it is for a nation on the brink of disaster or for an individual who shelters within his body an unsaved soul.

Wicked Hearts

On one occasion this same prophet laid bare the condition of the human heart in these words:

The heart is deceitful above all things
and beyond cure (Jer. 17:9).

How exactly he stated the case! God has put reins on the human heart to check its excesses of evil, but time and again it has broken away into almost unrestrained wickedness when His hand has slackened but a little.

Can one forget the tragic record of man in the time of Noah? "Every inclination of the thoughts of his heart was only evil all the time" (Gen. 6:5). It has been like that from Noah's day to the present. By nature would not all of us be like the people of Jerusalem—with hearts of shame, hearts of hopelessness, unwashed hearts?

Unsaved Souls

Except the heart be washed, the soul cannot be saved. Today people can no more partake of the salvation of God without the washing of their wicked hearts than could Israel of old. It was a God of *holiness* who repeatedly exhorted His people, "Be *holy.*" Of the same God, an inspired author wrote, "Your eyes are too pure to look on evil" (Hab. 1:13). It was said of God when He came in the flesh in the person of the divine Son that He hated iniquity. The same Lord and Christ will one day say to many who knock at the portals of the everlasting Kingdom, "I never knew you. Away from me, you evildoers! "(Matt. 7:23)

There is no room in heaven for idolators, thieves and drunkards. There is no room because wicked hearts have given birth to ungodly acts, and such hearts are in every way antithetical to all that heaven is. "Who may stand in his holy place?" asks the psalmist. "He who has clean hands and a pure heart" (Psa. 24:3, 4) is the answer.

An unwashed heart, therefore, means an unsaved soul!

Vain Efforts

Though people are largely indifferent as to the state of their souls, it is yet true that after a fashion many of them assent to the fact that some preparation is necessary before they meet God in judgment. They are aware that their present state of righteousness does not commend them to God, and so they go about to weed the gardens of their lives, to pull out the grass between the rows, and to cultivate and prune the plants that are left. Though drunkards, they stay sober long enough to attend church now and then. Though dishonest, they refrain from practicing deception in their own little circle of friends. Though covetous, they work to gain a reputation for generosity. But their efforts are in vain. The plants they have allowed to remain will never produce acceptable fruit. Though large and sturdy, they are but weeds themselves. Their hearts remain unwashed.

There are others who assent to their own unworthiness and energetically labor to make their lives clean. They fight against their own weaknesses. They try to bring their bodies into subjection. They strive earnestly toward the goal of moral perfection. But they never arrive! Nor have they so much as entered on the right path toward that end. Their hearts are unwashed.

They are like those of whom God spoke when He said,

> *Although you wash yourself with soda*
> *and use an abundance of soap,*
> *the stain of your guilt is still before me.*

Like the Pharisees, they have not learned that a cleansing of the *outside* of the cup is of no avail. If the heart is unwashed, it doesn't matter how sincere the effort to cleanse the outer life. Sinful acts spring from sinful hearts. A polluted fountain can never give forth sweet waters. Labor as one may to discipline his body in the interests of righteousness, he is doomed to utter failure.

Cleansed Natures

What then? Is there no hope? O yes! Wicked hearts may be washed, but only by the Great Fuller. No matter how corrupt his heart, the sinner can cry to the God of mercy and forgiveness:

> *Wash away all my iniquity*
>   *and cleanse me from my sin . . .*
> *Create in me a pure heart! (Psa. 51:2, 10).*

The apostle Paul could look out on a company of believers, recall their past lives of shame, and praise God for the change in their lives, for they had been washed, sanctified and justified in the name of the Lord Jesus and by the Spirit of God, who had set them free from the law of sin and death.

What humans cannot do, God can do! Heart washing is impossible with men, but the God who demands it also accomplishes it. O that people would recognize the futility of trying to cleanse their own hearts and petition the Fuller on High to wash away the scarlet stain of iniquity and make them white as snow.

> There is a fountain filled with blood,
>   Drawn from Immanuel's veins;
> And sinners, plunged beneath that flood,
>   Lose all their guilty stains.

Then, and only then, will wicked hearts be pure. Then, and only then, can dwellers in the Jerusalem of uncleanness taste of the salvation of God.

5

Backslidden People

JEREMIAH 3:22-25

A noted preacher voiced the conviction that once a man believed in Christ and knew the protecting care of the everlasting arms of the Father, he might slide a long way yet he could never slide all the way out. The relapse of such a person into periods of loose living and indifference may well be termed "backsliding."

God, however, was talking about something else when He spoke through the prophet Jeremiah in pleading voice saying,

> *Return, faithless people;*
> *I will cure you of backsliding.*

He was addressing godless children of godly parents, covenant breakers who might have availed themselves of covenant promises but who had not done so. The great mass of those to whom He spoke had never given their hearts to the true and living God nor honored His name. They were backsliders in the sense that they had turned from the worship of their fathers' God and fallen away to the abominations of idolatry.

They would have much company if they were living today. Any minister of the gospel may well testify to that fact, for there are numbers of men and women in his parish who have grown up in Christian homes but have never believed in the Son of God. Some of them, out of custom, religiously attend the services of the church, but their hearts are far from God. Others have long since ceased to have anything to do with the church. They are backslidden people.

One End

Skies are not always fair for such a person. As a human grasshopper, he may fiddle away the best years of his life, carefree and unconcerned. People may count him happy. But there is one sure end for a backslider—and only one! Sooner or later he must awaken to the realization that he is bankrupt before God. His conscience was once enlightened to know the truth of God; it will not let him go down to the grave in peace.

Like the man who has heard the good news and professedly believed in Christ, his end is often most miserable. Consider the story of Sabat, the Arabian. Sabat responded to the missionary efforts of the Rev. H. Martyn, then apostatized and took up the pen to defend Mohammedanism. One day the questions of another minister of the cross searched his heart, and he cried out, "I am unhappy. I have a mountain of burning sand on my head. When I go about, I know not what I am doing."

There is no profit in the lives of backslidden people. One of them forsook the covenant and turned his back on the faith of a believing father and a saintly mother. He entered one of the great western universities and sought the association of unregenerate youth in one of the fraternities. A Saturday night dance lasted on into the Lord's Day. Passers-by found his body, with that of a companion, near the wreck of an auto beside the road. Eternity had claimed a lost soul.

The God who knows the human heart pictured in fancy the response of penitents to His invitation to backsliders. Listen:

> *From our youth shameful gods have consumed*
> *the fruits of our fathers' labor—*
> *their flocks and herds,*
> *their sons and daughters (v. 24).*

These are words put on the lips of second-generation despisers of God's covenant with Israel. They constitute the confession of those who had themselves experienced the folly and unfruitfulness of apostasy as they had also seen it in the lives of their fathers. Life for them had proved to be vain and unsatisfying. It had brought only misery and despair.

One Hope

There is no blacker picture conceivable. They were without God and without hope. Nothing to live for! Nothing of hope in death! Borne in deep upon their conscience was the solemn truth of the everlasting God: "What good is it for a man to gain the whole world, yet forfeit his soul?" (Mark 8:36).

Did I say "without hope"? Yes, but thanks be to God there *was* yet hope, a sure and steadfast hope. By divine grace they might yet lay hold on this hope. It is a glorious hope. It is good news. It is music in the ear of a despairing backslider. Like a clarion call it rings across field and dale. It penetrates far into mountain recesses. It awakens those who slumber. The concerned backslider listens:

> *Surely in the Lord our God*
> *is the salvation of Israel (v. 23).*

So Jeremiah preached, and so some of the backslidden people of Israel laid hold on this hope and were saved.

I have a word for backsliders: What was your home like? Did Christian parents lovingly provide that you should have opportunity to know of divine love that prompted Almighty God to send His dear Son into a world of shame that He might purchase salvation for those who were wayward? And have you never taken this Christ to be your Savior in answer to their prayers?

There is only one hope for the backslider. It is not to be found in Gautama or Mohammed or in the religions they have left behind them. One seeks in vain to accomplish his own salvation by deeds of kindness and mercy and discipline of character. That hope is in God's Son, and in Him alone; it is a hope that does not fade away.

One Way

The nature of hope, however, is strange. Unless it is embraced, it often ceases to be hope and becomes condemnation instead. And unless backsliders reach out by faith and take to themselves the hope that the Lord holds before them, they become acquainted with the truth of this assertion.

But how can they make this hope their own? There is one way— and only one! It appears in God's impersonation of the penitents: "We have sinned against the Lord our God." In other words, the way is *confession*.

Kinds of Confession

In our modern world there are three outstanding kinds of confession. One is a cheap variety. It consists of pouring out the shame of one's life before his fellow men. It is the Buchmanite type. The second kind of confession is a mistaken one. It is the revelation before an earthly priest of one's sinful actions. It ignores the teaching of the Bible that there is *only one* mediator between God and man, the Lord Jesus Christ.

Obviously it must be another kind of confession that constitutes the way by which backslidden people may become reconciled to the Heavenly Father. We analyze the confession they make. It is humble and it deals with sin. Addressed to God, it recognizes that sin is an offense against Him. It professes helplessness. It invites grace.

O that today's backslidden people would turn from the end that awaits them! O that they would consider the hope that lies in the good news of the vicarious sacrifice of God's Son and open their hearts in repentant confession to the God of forgiveness and grace! He is ready to receive repentant backsliders and make them His own.

6

The Latter End of a Sinner
JEREMIAH 4:30

One night at a late hour on a dimly lit street in the metropolitan Boston area, a drunken woman emerged from within a modern saloon, staggered a few steps unsteadily, and fell to the sidewalk. No one within the saloon cared about her plight. Passers-by helped her to regain her feet. They heard her mumble between sobs a defense of her own respectability, though they did not believe her words. She was gaily dressed—too gaily. Her face was painted, though not enough to conceal the marks of sin. A squad car drove up, and two policemen took her from the scene. It was a brief drama but a vivid one.

How like God's description of the latter end of a sinner! That picture, the first reference of which was to a nation that had forsaken the Lord of heaven and earth and allied itself with sinful, idolatrous peoples, is found in the thirtieth verse of the fourth chapter of Jeremiah's prophecy:

> *What are you doing, O devastated one?*
>   *Why dress yourself in scarlet*
>   *and put on jewels of gold?*
> *Why shade your eyes with paint?*
>   *You adorn yourself in vain.*
> *Your lovers despise you;*
>   *they seek your life.*

With what exactness do the words describe the latter end of a nation that had preferred sin to righteousness, yet how akin they are to such a circumstance as that outlined above! They show the sad fate of a sinner who has just come to the realization that sin has no more pleasure to offer and, instead, unsmilingly compels a miserable servitude and open shame.

Spoiled!

For a long time Judah had been playing the harlot. Her heart was not in the worship supposedly accorded to the God of her fathers in the temple rites and sacrifices. The hearts of rulers and people alike were far from the God of truth and grace. Sinful practices abounded. Immorality and injustice prevailed. The public policy was one of reliance upon ungodly neighbors, of rebellion against the Lord and His requirements. His prophets were beaten and killed; their admonitions were disregarded; their counsel was rejected. Judah had not only sunk deeply into sin, but also it had chosen companions of sin. Her "lovers" were of ill repute in the sight of God.

Now, though the kingdom yet remained intact, its foundations had been severely undermined. Like termite-ridden timbers, they needed but the slightest blow to send the whole structure toppling. Sin had eaten away at every point—in temple, palace, court of law, private dealings, and personal practice of religion. Judah was spoiled, though she knew it not. Soon the awful awakening would come!

There are men and women who are fast approaching the point of being spoiled and who do not know it. There are young men and young women who are flirting with sin, ignoring God, His Word and His church and taking to themselves other lovers. Pleasure is bright and alluring. It screens the latter end of a life apart from God. Its victims laugh at the thought that the trail ends where a fallen woman lies sobbing on the dark, shadowed sidewalk. Yet sometimes it is there; sometimes it is in the swirling waters and jagged rocks beneath a high bridge; sometimes it is in a closet of shame and remorse; sometimes it is on a deathbed of woe. Sinners come to their bitter end—*spoiled!*

Desperate!

Judah's ambassadors had been very busy. Reckless and inconstant in fidelity, the nation had pledged loyalty now to Assyria, now to Egypt. These "lovers" had taken what they could get from her. She flattered herself that her cleverness or attractiveness had procured her own preservation while countries round about had been spoiled by hostile armies. Even her own sister kingdom to the north had fallen beneath the attack of marauding hosts. As for herself, she could still be bold and gleeful.

Jeremiah was not so optimistic. A day was soon to come in which disaster would overtake Jerusalem and its environs. The surety of impending doom would somehow communicate itself to national leaders. They would resort to the old methods of providing security. Diplomatic juggling, the promise of tribute, commercial concessions—surely some of these would tempt her past "lovers." Surely she need not fear! But disaster was sure to approach, and all her overtures, though bold, could scarcely disguise her intuitive sense of desperation.

How often have those who have followed the way of sin come to a similar plight! They have long been successful in hiding their sin from parents and friends. They have been able to preserve a good reputation. Their gloss of respectability has not been penetrated. They have been able to bridle their sin instead of being bridled by it. Then has come a time when they are dimly aware that they are slipping, when they see the handwriting on the wall, when they begin to feel the iron hand of sin crushing their wills. They do not admit defeat, however. Rather, they stake everything on their ability to appease the demands Satan makes upon them.

Forsaken!

Yes, everything is staked, but tragedy has long lurked around the corner, and suddenly it closes in triumphantly to seize its prey. The little Palestinian kingdom found it so. One "lover" deserted her and sought the safety of his own castle behind broad defenses. The other, like a ruthless murderer, broke down the walls of her home, killed some of her children, put out the eyes of others, assailed her person, and dragged her, torn and bleeding, to a distant land to be his slave.

So it is with the false lover of men's souls, the Prince of Darkness. He takes tribute until there is no more to be given and the treasury is spoiled. Then he spurns every effort toward appeasement. He becomes a merciless master. His true character becomes apparent. He is not a prince of delight but an enemy and a deceiver. The attractive wages he once paid are found to be counterfeit money—utterly valueless. His only real interest was to enslave his victim to ignominious, eternal servitude. Would his slaves but speak the truth, they would say that it is so.

That is not the end of the *gross* sinner alone. It is the latter end awaiting *all* sinners. Does one cherish within his heart a secret love for some seemingly inoffensive sin? The history of Judah shows that she did not immediately lapse into open idolatry. If the heart is unguarded, that seemingly unimportant sin may be working ever so slowly the undoing of body and soul. Does the sin of unbelief govern the affections? Has self become as God? Is there pride, jealousy, envy, backbiting? Is there just plain unconcern about the soul's salvation? If so, I read with trembling in God's Word the terrible description of the latter end. Jeremiah's question is pertinent: "What are you doing, O devastated one? . . . Your lovers despise you; they seek your life."

Long years ago the True Lover of men's souls hung on a cruel cross to save sinners from the latter end of earthly misery that must necessarily await them and also to save them from the final wages of sin, eternal death. The gospel of His redeeming love invites everyone to receive His pardoning grace and to put away forever the sin that is slowly, surely, perhaps without awareness, leading down a road that has a bitter ending, possibly to an end not unlike that of the unwanted woman, sobbing in her drunkenness, victim of her own sin.

7

Spiritual Illiterates
JEREMIAH 5:21-24

"Hear this, you foolish and senseless people,
  who have eyes but do not see,
  who have ears but do not hear:
Should you not fear me?" declares the Lord.
  "Should you not tremble in my presence?
I made the sand a boundary for the sea,
  an everlasting barrier it cannot cross.
The waves may roll, but they cannot prevail;
  they may roar, but they cannot cross it.
But these people have stubborn and rebellious hearts;
  they have turned aside and gone away.
They do not say to themselves,
  'Let us fear the Lord our God,
who gives autumn and spring rains in season,
  who assures us of the regular weeks of harvest.'"

Although we have much sympathy for a man who cannot read because his eyes are sightless, our attitude is much different toward one who has never learned to read because of laziness or stubbornness. In a country where everyone has an opportunity to learn to read and write, illiteracy is regarded as an inexcusable tragedy. Spiritual illiteracy is little different. God is not sparing in His denunciation of those who have had a chance to know Him and His salvation but have despised the opportunity.

The Book God has given us and which we know as the Bible is perhaps not quite so simple as some would have us believe. To know it as God originally gave it through men moved by the Holy Spirit, one must be a student of Greek, Hebrew and Aramaic. Few of us are thus qualified. Also, great scholars have been baffled to understand fully some portions of the Book. Is God then justified in condemning those who do not seek with all their hearts to come to a knowledge of Him by diligent reading of the Scriptures?

The answer is commonly given by Christian people that the essential saving truths of the Word are simple enough to be received into the heart of a child and embraced by his mind. This is true enough. But I would invite you to consider with me the problem of spiritual illiteracy from a much different point of view.

Men have not always had alphabets of letters which they could put together to form words. The writing of ancient Egypt was at first nothing but pictures that suggested actions or situations and so conveyed messages to those who looked at them. From this simple beginning developed the hieroglyphs, picture writing with which the many archaeological discoveries of recent years have made us familiar. So it is that we become aware of the fact that the simplest book is not the one which is printed in words and letters.

God's Picture Book

The simplest book is a picture book. Children read such books long before they are able to recognize and interpret words. They get the message, though not always in the same words. If only God had such a book, surely His condemnation of spiritual illiteracy would be manifestly justified.

He does! Unlike His other Book, the Bible, this book does not need to be translated into many tongues. It speaks one language to all men. There are two major divisions in it. Both are pictorial, but one is more like a moving picture, while the other's pictures are for the most part still. The latter group of pictures is made up of the things God has made—the earth and all its physical wonders and the starry heavens above. The moving pictures are those of the hand of God at work in controlling and operating the forces of nature that He has established and that He makes subservient to the needs of men. The two parts of this book of God are known as "Creation" and "Providence."

Providence

The words of our meditation are concerned with the second part of God's picture book, "Providence." Has not God spoken in the pictures of His providence? Powerful tides that man has never been able to harness mark the ebb and flow of ocean waters. Fierce storms rage at sea and billows rise like mountains with valleys between. Earthquakes shake the bed of the deep. But behold how God speaks in the picture of providence, for He has "made the sand a boundary for the sea, an everlasting barrier it cannot cross." He who reads must assent that "all things are possible with God."

Have you taken thought as to the rain that drops from heaven? Should it be dispatched by a capricious hand, it might come in great floods or be withheld entirely in the growing season. One year might see a superabundance of moisture; the next might find the whole earth victim of a great drought. But God sends the sunshine and rain according to the measure of the earth's needs. He puts bridles upon the clouds, and each day marches the sun around its circuit. Yes, He "gives autumn and spring rains in season." In the picture of providence one reads of His wisdom and goodness and power.

"If winter come, can spring be far behind?" We know that the woodland violets and triliums and the marshland cowslips follow the showers of April. With the July sun, the farmer is raking the hay in his meadow. Midsummer invariably witnesses the fields of grain turning to brown and gold. These are pictures of providence, for He "assures us of the regular weeks of harvest." God's picture book in this way speaks to us of His sovereignty over all the earth, His faithfulness, and His unchanging love in making regular provision for the material needs of His people.

As we read this picture book of God, it ought to keep us humble. As it teaches us of His mighty power, His excellent greatness, His perfect holiness, His unchanging decrees, and His great grace, we ought to be filled with awe. A holy fear should flood our souls. We should worship Him in all reverence. We should be aware of His eternal power and Godhead. We should cast all idols from us.

Unmoved by the Message

The tragedy is that many are unmoved by all these things. They ignore or misread the book. Some are like the early decipherers of Hittite inscriptions; each had a different interpretation of the materials. Some are like the artist who is not concerned with understanding the message of the hieroglyph but only desires to drink in the aesthetic perfume of the bird and animal forms that appear in the writing.

God's chosen people in the land of Judah had long been unmoved by the book's message. Their fathers had taught them to read it during the period of their infancy. Prophet after prophet had reminded them of its message. They had chosen to forget. They had preferred not to listen. Now God points out their folly and gives them one last opportunity to hearken.

I have a neighbor who is a lover of nature. He drinks in the beauty of flowers. He loves to make his way to unfrequented mountain summits. He watches with anticipation the unfolding of the plants in his garden. Exclamations of wonder escape his lips as he beholds nature's grandeur. Yet he does not honor God as the Author of creation and the Controller of providence. He has misread God's picture book.

Moreover, he is under the condemnation of God, for as God pronounced the inhabitants of Judah "foolish," so he declares all who misread or ignore the book "without excuse" (Rom. 1:20).

If He thus judges those who have access only to this *simple* book, how much more severe must be His judgment on those who have the Bible as well and who remain willfully blind to its teaching! What a pity that anyone who has *both* books of his revelation should remain spiritually illiterate and die in his sins! Thank God, there is an alternative. As the sinner reads in the picture book of God's eternal power and Godhead and in the Book of books of the gracious salvation to be found in the Crucified One, he can call on the Spirit who is the Divine Interpreter to take away his blindness and enable him to read clearly and with faith. Submitting himself humbly to that same life-giving Spirit, he can make that salvation his own.

8

At the Crossroads

JEREMIAH 6:16

This is what the Lord says:
Stand at the crossroads and look;
*   ask for the ancient paths,*
ask where the good way is, and walk in it,
*   and you will find rest for your souls.*
But you said, "We will not walk in it."

There is a screeching of brakes. A high-powered car comes to a stop. The driver emerges from the car and mounts the rickety steps to the porch of the crossroads store. "I say," he begins, addressing the group of loungers, "which of these roads goes to Canton?"

An old farmer speaks up: "Sir, I reckon they all do. That black top to the right is a new road and good for a ways, but I wouldn't trust it farther on. The one to the left was built just a few years ago. It will get you there, but it was cheap construction, and the frost has hit it pretty hard. If I was you, stranger, I'd go straight on. It's a little farther, and it's not quite so modern a road, but it was built to last."

The driver, impatient, is halfway down the steps before the old man has finished. "Well, grandpa," he calls over his shoulder, "you're not me. I'm taking the blacktop."

God's Counsel

A people at the crossroads were privileged to listen to counsel from their God. They were the people of Judah. From of old their nation had been unique in that it worshiped a God who dwelt in a temple not made with hands, eternal in the heavens. It was under covenant obligation to render obedience to an exacting moral code, the Decalogue. One can well imagine that such a religion was not always popular. Self-reliant individuals would prefer to work out the problems of the nation by themselves without the direction of a covenant God. Licentious persons would rebel at the stringent morality required. Those weak in faith would prefer gods that they could see and handle.

So it was that the chosen people stood at the crossroads not once but many times, debating whether they should remain loyal to the faith of their fathers and continue to walk in the old paths or follow some new form of teaching that would be more acceptable.

It was at such a time that they heard the voice of the Lord their God: "*Stand at* the crossroads and look; ask for the ancient paths, ask where the good way is, and walk in it, and you will find rest for your souls."

It was good advice. Counseling careful thought and consideration, it pointed out a proven path. It promised rest at the end of the trail.

Perhaps the religion of Abraham, Isaac and Jacob did seem to some to be at times outmoded, but before Judah tossed it lightly overboard it would have been well for her to do a bit of evaluating. She was only an insignificant people, yet God had redeemed her when she was a slave nation. He had blessed her in giving her material prosperity and deliverance from enemies. Would the so-called gods of the nations do as much? Would it pay in the long run to sacrifice righteousness for the sake of having a good time?

Judah's Answer

Judah did not care! She was a wanton child. She did not want her Lord's advice. This was her answer: "We will not walk in it." This was rebellion! This was willful sin! This was open apostasy! Like the driver of the high-powered car, she had made a perverse choice. She did not know that tragedy lurked ahead, that the God she was forsaking would forsake her and leave her to be set upon by powerful foes and spoiled. The driver who started out on the blacktop did not know that on a stony stretch in the road ahead a blowout caused by a bruised tire would send his car hurtling from the highway, and that his own body would be crushed in the wreckage. All he either knew or cared about at the moment was that new paths seemed attractive.

I am sure you agree with me that Judah's choice was a foolish one, yet the situation in our own nation is not far different. We in America are proud—too proud. It were well that we listen to Him who says, "Nevertheless, I have a few things against you" (Rev. 2:14). Have we profited by the example of ancient Judah? We must not be unaware of those searching words: "*Stand at* the crossroads and look; ask for the ancient paths, ask where the good way is, and walk in it, and you will find rest for your souls."

Our Answer

Twentieth century America is not exactly given to *thought and consideration.* Our tendency is to act first. Perhaps we think afterward—perhaps not. We are prone to say, "Columbus took a chance; so will I." We forget that Columbus engaged in careful reflection and did some serious planning.

Twentieth century America is not exactly given to *following the proven way.* We are like the Athenians of old. We lend our ears to the hearing of "the latest ideas." We want adventure, and because we cannot be explorers and world travelers we gratify our desires by psychologically identifying ourselves with the hero of the drama, novel or movie. We are happiest when we are out upon uncharted courses and along unbeaten paths.

Twentieth century America is not exactly given to interest in *rest.* Activity, intense activity, is her best characterization. No won-

der our journalists sometimes speak of "mad America." The thought
of rest does not appeal until we suddenly awaken to the fact that
the strength and vitality of youth are gone, no more to be re-
claimed. Then we often discover that the rest we desire is beyond
our ability to obtain.

The Church's Answer

There are not many churches that have discontinued the singing
of "Faith of Our Fathers," but comparatively few really mean what
they sing. Another religion, modern liberalism, has gained the as-
cendancy in many quarters. It is not found along the "ancient paths";
it branches out in almost every way into an unsurveyed wasteland
where there is nothing of spiritual food, nothing to quench the
soul's thirst, a trackless space in which its victims die, far from
home.

The "ancient paths" knew only one way of salvation, faith in a
Savior who loved His own and gave Himself for them in vicarious
death upon the cross, bearing the sins of His people and meriting
for them forgiveness and eternal life. But the new religion, really an
old religion in a new form, offers a different way of salvation from
that found in the "ancient paths." It says to men, "Do the best you
can. Do good. Help the poor and unfortunate. Work out your own
salvation without help from God. Anyway, God is love and surely
He will not visit you with condemnation."

The "ancient paths" acquainted men with a Book from God, trustworthy in all its parts. The new religion has a book, but a much
smaller one, and it does not consider this book as being from God
any more than are other worthwhile books.

The "ancient paths" counseled men to tell the story of the Lamb
Who was sent to take away the sin of the world. The new religion
sends men to the heathen to teach them better methods of agricul-
ture and modern systems of sanitation—little more.

God's counsel has been brought to our attention. We know how
Judah answered. We know her unhappy fate. God says:

> *"Ask for the ancient paths,*
> *ask where the good way is, and walk in it."*

9

One's Boasting
JEREMIAH 9:23, 24

W hat makes one rejoice? People have been known to exult in their own wickedness. Some are content when their pride is fostered. Some glory in achievement. Tell me, in what do *you* glory? I am concerned because God has said through His prophet Jeremiah:

> *Let not the wise man boast of his wisdom*
> *or the strong man boast of his strength*
> *or the rich man boast of his riches,*
> *but let him who boasts boast about this:*
> *that he understands and knows me,*
> *that I am the Lord, who exercises kindness,*
> *justice and righteousness on earth,*
> *for in these I delight.*

Spoken so long ago, these words have never found their way to the basket of discarded phrases. They constitute a timeless gem of revelation that each succeeding generation may well receive as a personal message from the almighty God. Perhaps they speak to *you*.

Unworthy Reasons

Wisdom, riches, power! In three words God has summed up the things on which those of the world rely. We were never more keenly aware of this fact than today.

Solomon put wisdom at the head of the list. It takes first place here. Solomon was right, too, for riches and power naturally follow where wisdom has gone on before. Yet the wisdom God now speaks of is somewhat different from that which Solomon coveted. For him, the fear of the Lord was the beginning of wisdom; in this other "wisdom," the Lord is not considered at all. This wisdom is akin to cleverness, to scheming, to careful planning.

Where are the leaders of nations today? They are closeted in the council chambers, planning, planning, planning! Some are considering how they may turn the tide of war and subjugate other peoples. Some are mapping out programs of neutral action. Some are calculating carefully how they may help their friends and yet avoid war for themselves. Some are scheming to make their defenses impregnable.

A Faulty Reliance

God is left out of the picture. The council chambers are not known as places of prayer. There is little serious effort to apply the principles of the Bible in international affairs. O yes, the name of God often appears in the great political speeches of kings and chancellors, of premiers and presidents, but one senses that this is more for effect than because of conviction. There is not much suggestion that the fear of the Lord is in any way connected with wisdom.

On one occasion a noted figure, in an address to the world, betrayed this fact when his only reference to God was that surely He would help those who helped themselves. Yes, I am quite convinced that the nations of the world are relying for the most part on a wisdom that reserves little place for God.

Reliance upon riches is hardly less noticeable. Soldiers stand guard at a fort in the Kentucky hills, because buried there is a great quantity of gold. It was bought at a dear price on the assumption that its possession would safeguard the economic supremacy of our country. Under circumstances that gave evidence of the fact that the continuance of a nation in battle today depends on its national wealth, a nation across the sea released to our government a detailed account of its own resources.

Perhaps more evident and tangible than glorying in wisdom or riches is glorying in power. Nation races against nation to produce more airplanes, more tanks, more guns, more warships, more submarines. The world is interested in might, not in right. It is trusting in man-made power, not in the power of God.

It is conceivable that a people might employ wisdom, riches and power in right causes and with the blessing of God, and perhaps that is true of some of the world powers at the present. Just so, a Christian doctor employs drugs and medicines with the prayer that God, if it be His will, may use them to restore the patient to health. The danger comes when God is forgotten and the doctor's trust rests in the medicines alone, or the nation's confidence does not reckon at all with God. The acid test comes when people are tempted to glory in wisdom and riches and power rather than in God, or to give them first place and call in God's help only as a last resort.

There was a period in history when the people of Judah did not make wisdom, riches and power their chief pride, but in the time of Jeremiah all was different. The national leaders were continually scheming to preserve their kingdom from destruction. They sought to buy deliverance with gold and silver, even though it meant robbing the temple of its sacred vessels. They switched allegiance from one nation to another, according to the rise or fall in power of those nations.

They were too proud or too faithless or too conscious of the broken covenant to plead their cause before God and ask His help. But their way was not the way of safety, as they thought. Instead, the things in which they gloried brought them to the edge of disaster, and in confusion they were plunged over the precipice by the hand of the power to which they had entrusted themselves.

A Just Cause

If only a just cause had occasioned their glorying! It is not sinful for us to glory. In fact, it would be sinful for us to exclude all glorying from our life. Sin is charged against us only when we take pride in that which is unworthy of glory.

We think of the apostle to the Gentiles. Paul's glorying was in the cross of Christ, and his entire life was given over to that glorying. At the thought of the cross and what it signified, joy welled up in his heart, though he was faced with uncertainty and perhaps death in a Roman prison. Again, that glorying prompted him to say to the people of Corinth, "I resolved to know nothing while I was with you except Jesus Christ and him crucified" (1 Cor. 2:2).

Did Paul, then, know the secret of the words entrusted to Jeremiah? Yes, for these were the words: "Let him who boasts boast about this: that he understands and knows me." Paul knew God through Him whom to know aright is life eternal. Paul had understanding, the kind that makes one aware of the truth that apart from God he or she can do nothing.

A Right Relationship

Paul did not care about the wisdom of the world. His life was dedicated to the preaching of a message that was foolishness in the eyes of the world. He did not care about money. He solicited for his own use no offerings from those among whom he labored, but put his hand to tent-making when his needs so required. He placed little value on human strength, relying on the power of God to open prison gates.

Is it possible that we who have been saved by the grace of our God should glory in anything else than that in which Paul gloried? We know Him who was rich but who, to rescue us, became poor that we might have true riches. We meditate on this truth only to confess that our cup is full and running over. In the consciousness of our fellowship with the Lord of Glory we find our hearts singing within us. Truly this is cause for exultation—to know the God who came to be among us and to give Himself for us.

10

A Humble Confession

JEREMIAH 10:23

*I know, O Lord, that a man's life is not his own;
it is not for man to direct his steps.*

The Lord Jesus once told the story of a man who was rich, yet who was a fool. An abundant harvest had filled his granaries to overflowing, and the man had determined to erect more capacious storehouses in their place. He was then resolved to put in store all the fruits that had been gathered, after which he would give himself to leisure and the material luxuries of life. No thought entered his mind that his plans would miscarry. With every feeling of security he embarked upon the determined program. "But God said to him, 'You fool! This very night your life will be demanded from you'" (Luke 12:20). Borne home to the rich fool in the twilight hour of his sojourn on earth was the truth, "A man's life is not his own."

Historical Background

An interesting historical setting produced the prayer in which confession of this fact was made. To a people who had long been living by the philosophy of the rich fool, God had at last made known the sure advance of a hostile army to plunder the kingdom and carry away the people into captivity. The destruction was prophesied as imminent. The prophet's words were alarming. There was no time to lose. The stoutest fortress would fall, and its inhabitants were urgently warned to pack their bundles in haste that they might be ready to leave in a moment.

The prophet was not slow to pursue his advantage. Before this time his admonitions had been unavailing, but now he would destroy once and for all that false sense of security that had made his countrymen proud and godless. With cutting satire he exposed the impotence of the idol gods in which they had long trusted. He declared the majestic power and greatness of the true God, whose wrath was now unleashed against the doers of iniquity. He denounced the religious leaders who had led their flocks astray, and he prophesied for them an unhappy end.

If his words should not bring the people to their senses, the harassing experiences of the invasion would, and in anticipation of a broken spirit on the part of the people, Jeremiah put into each mouth words of confession: "*I know,* O Lord, that a man's life is not his own; it is not for man to direct his steps."

Human Inability

Nothing was further from Judah's desire than to suffer invasion, to have her national existence destroyed, and to go away into a long exile. But what could she do? She was helpless. It was plain that the destinies of men and of nations were held in the hand of a higher power.

It had always been that way. Day after day the very sight of the champion of the Philistines incited greater fear in the hearts of the Israelites. Not one dared to go forth to meet him. Then one day, David, a shepherd boy, resolute in faith, slew the mighty Goliath, enemy of Israel.

Alexander the Great built up a massive empire only to die almost before the blush of youth had faded from his countenance. The great Roman conqueror Caesar was cut off from the enjoyment of his victories when the trusted hand of Brutus plunged a dagger into his breast.

In World War II we saw Norway fall in a day and witnessed the collapse of the supposedly impregnable Maginot Line. Are we yet unconvinced of the limitations that check the ability of people to work out their own destiny?

What is true of nations and generals is true of every individual in the common walk of life. The words of the poet might well have been those of the rich fool: "I am the master of my fate! I am the captain of my soul!" But what utter folly to arrogate such power to oneself!

He who speaks in this way knows nothing of what lies ahead in life's pathway. Strength may be his today, but tomorrow those who have had strong physiques and sturdy health will lie for the first time on hospital beds. Tomorrow wealthy citizens will find themselves in poverty. Tomorrow a nation's once-honored leaders will face the firing squad.

If people have no certain control over their lives in this world, much less can they depend on their own powers to carry them safely out into eternity. How can we direct our steps down the highway of salvation? According to the Scriptures, we are dead in trespasses and sins. How idle is the boast of those who think to lift themselves into heaven by their own bootstraps! "It is not for man to direct his steps."

Divine Control

Scripture warrants us in assuming that the opposite of "for man" is "for God," and the context in which our meditation is found gives us license to interpret the prayer of confession in this way: "It is not for man to direct his steps; rather, it is for God to direct them."

It was a Babylonian army that swept in to devastate the land of Judah—an army used of God as a chastening rod to bring His wayward people to repentance. God was later to punish the Babylonians for their own wickedness. God directed the hand of David as he released the stone from his sling in the fight with Goliath. God humbled the proud Nebuchadnezzar and caused his removal from his kingdom. And we may well rest assured that God's decrees determined the rise and fall of Alexander, Caesar and Napoleon.

A young man preparing for the ministry was willing to admit that God's decrees have governed the fortunes of *some* men in history, but he was unwilling to grant that they control the individual destinies of *all* people. Was he right? What of the ordinary person? Is it true that God directs *his* steps?

People make plans. They set their wills. They decide on courses of action. But God "works out everything in conformity with the purpose of his will"(Eph. 1:11). Sometimes His direction of men's steps consists in allowing them to follow out their own plans, whether they be for good or for bad. Sometimes He overrules and forcibly restrains them from carrying out their purposes. Sometimes He moves them to repentance so that they reverse the choices they have made. In any case, this direction of man's steps rests in the hand of the Almighty.

Divine Direction

In spiritual matters this truth is even more apparent. It is God's quickening, the regenerating power of the Holy Spirit, that establishes one on the highway of salvation, and it is God who works in the born-again life that such a life may will and act "according to his good purpose" (Phil. 2:13). Little wonder that Paul exclaimed about his Lord that "from him and through him and to him are all things" (Rom. 11:36)!

The humble confession of the people of Judah came too late to stave off the disaster that threatened them. Those who were spared immediate death died in a strange land. Their children and many of their grandchildren died on foreign soil. How great a pity it was that they did not long before confess their own inability and plead for grace and help from the God of lovingkindness and tender mercy!

Would that the tragedy were an isolated occurrence in history, but it is not. There are and always have been proud hearts that refuse to submit to the sovereign God. They echo and reecho the words: "I am the master of my fate! I am the captain of my soul!"

O that every such spirit might be broken and that every heart might exclaim, "*Your* will be done!" For if one willfully cleaves to his own course and God lets him die in his sin, there will be no hope for him on the day of judgment. Some day every knee will bow and every tongue confess, but as in the case of Judah the time for confession leading to safety will be past. "*Now* is the day of salvation" (2 Cor. 6:2), and it is God's direction of one's steps in *this* life that will determine his blessedness forever.

11

God Deals with Disobedience

JEREMIAH 11:7, 8

From the time I brought your forefathers up from Egypt until today, I warned them again and again, saying, "Obey me." But they did not listen or pay attention; instead, they followed the stubbornness of their evil hearts. So I brought on them all the curses of the covenant I had commanded them to follow but that they did not keep.

The duty of obedience is a subject to which children and adults alike commonly listen with distaste, even with rebellion. As long as it harbors sin, the human heart will never love obedience to God. Just as in the case of our first parents, sin and disobedience go hand in hand. Only a miracle of grace can cause a reversal of attitude and bring about a love for obedience. When the preacher said to his congregation, "Brothers and sisters, whatever the good Lord tells me to do in His blessed Book, that is what I'm

53

going to do," we can be quite certain that God's grace had transformed his heart.

His Instructions

In that same "blessed Book," God has specifically directed people what to do and what not to do. There is nothing vague about His requirements. Some things He commands; other things He forbids. Indeed, it would be a Herculean task to attempt the tabulation of all the things either allowed or prohibited in the Word. Each separate command is of importance, and we do well to search the Scriptures that we may know just what God requires of us.

Occasionally, however, God's instructions to us are brought within the compass of a single statement and, for the moment, the individual requirements are lost to sight. The burden of the message entrusted by God to the prophets was often of this type. In Jeremiah 11:7 the text of the message is found. No words are wasted. It is comprehensive, brief, to the point. This is what God says: "Obey me."

After all, the important thing is a heart attitude of obedience, for if the heart's resolve is to obey God's voice, the individual will be ready for any specific command or request God may address to him. Like a pure fountain that sends forth only clear, sweet waters, a heart that is tuned to obedience will produce obedience at the various points tested. Or, like the regenerate nature that cannot but issue in good works, its fruit will be conformity to each expression of the divine will.

If only we might learn to obey God! That is what God wants. As revealed by Samuel's denunciation of Saul's disobedience, to obey is better in the Lord's sight than sacrifice (1 Sam. 15:22). Nor is it only what God *wants;* it is also His *due.* Moral responsibility was emphasized in Peter's affirmation: "We must obey God rather than men!" (Acts 5:29). "Ought" today is a neglected word, but it is neglected only because of the general apostasy of our age. It should be revived, and it should be applied to the filial obedience due our Heavenly Father, for He is indeed the great Sovereign of the universe. We belong to Him. All we have has come from Him. He gives us life and sustains that life. He sent His Son to purchase our salvation. He directs us by His Spirit. We *ought* to *obey* Him!

The command was not a new one in Jeremiah's day. No, he was one of the last of the prophets. Jeremiah preached from the text "Obey me," but so had the many prophets before him. What we read in his memoirs is that God had communicated the same instructions to Israel ever since they had found deliverance from Egyptian bondage. Every prophet had preached obedience to God. That message had been emphasized and reemphasized. God's servants had diligently proclaimed His desire for an obedient people. He Himself had been greatly concerned in the matter, for we read that He "warned them again and again."

His Warning

The tragedy was that the command "Obey me" did not seem to have borne much fruit. When a God-fearing sovereign came to the throne, most of his time was occupied in trying to undo the acts of disobedience on the part of his predecessors. Pagan altars had to be broken down; pagan images had to be destroyed. There was little time left for a program of implanting the desire for obedience in the individual heart. As a result, obeying God had not become entirely habitual with Israel. Once in a great while, the lesson of obedience would appear to have been learned, only to have the succeeding generation become more sinful in that respect than ever. And so God said to Jeremiah, "They did not listen or pay attention."

Like so many today, they were interested in other things. They much preferred a religion in which they could make their own choices, an easier religion, more ceremonial, less moral in character. They liked gods who did not point out their sins, who did not issue commands, who did not require obedience—gods who could neither see, nor hear, nor punish them for disobedience.

God's charge against Israel, however, was more severe than a mere charge of negligence or of following the easy path. He declared the chosen people stubborn in "their evil hearts." They were rebellious against their Maker. They had hardened their hearts. They were hostile toward God, loving wickedness instead.

Therefore God says that Israel had knowingly, willingly, actively, stubbornly disobeyed Him, preferring sin and disobedience to righteousness and obedience. It seems a serious charge to declare that people about us who refuse to obey God are like this, but we live in an age when culture and courtesy cover up the real attitudes of people's hearts. It is only in unguarded moments or in times of great stress that they betray their real feelings. Perhaps even in Jeremiah's time the neighbors of idolaters and sinners would not have done so, but the God who knows the human heart made that very charge.

His Judgment

Israel was to learn that God executes judgment against those who refuse to obey Him. Because she turned a deaf ear to the instructions laid before her by the Lord, God informed Jeremiah that she would bring upon herself the curses of a broken covenant. Her kingdom would be despoiled. The people would be taken captive and pressed into slavery. They would be scattered over the earth. And Jeremiah lived to witness the truth of God's words.

We are prone to hope that God will be like the modern indulgent parent and that there will be no reckoning if we, also, disobey Him. It is a vain hope. Judgment is sure to come. As God punished Israel, so will He punish *all* whose hearts are confirmed in disobedience toward Him. Let us never think otherwise. "A man reaps what he sows" (Gal. 6:7).

What would God have me say to those who disobey? I think it has to be something like this: "I could admonish you not to steal, not to kill, not to lie, but I would rather write upon your hearts that all-inclusive command of God: 'Obey Me.' I urge you to repudiate that disobedient heart and to obey the sovereign God, not only for the sake of your own happiness, but also for the sake of Him who came in love to woo the disobedient to Himself. Won't you obey God? He wants you to obey. Why not start the day—every day—with the promise that, with His help, you will?"

12

Enemies and Grace
JEREMIAH 12:16

I t is common for men to think of an enemy only as an enemy. In southern mountain feuds there is no thought of reconciliation and no suggestion of love or compassion. Enmity passes down from generation to generation. To forget it or to give it up would be an unforgivable act of dishonor.

How different is God's attitude toward those who have constituted themselves enemies against Him and His people! They are invited to taste of His grace and to share the blessings of His covenant. Divine love toward enemies of God is attested by such New Testament passages as Romans 5:10—"When we were God's enemies, we were reconciled to him though the death of his Son." Yet the Old Testament, also, is rich in offers of grace to the estranged sinner. Consider, for example, Jeremiah 12:16—

> *And if they learn well the ways of my people and swear by my name, saying, "As surely as the Lord lives"—even as they once taught my people to swear by Baal—then they will be established among my people.*

God did not become a God of grace with the coming of Christ. His nature did not differ from Abraham's time to the time of Jeremiah. It has not changed from Jeremiah's day to the present. Our God is an unchanging God, the same in all ages, and His mercy endures forever. As was wicked Cain at the very dawn of history, so the enemies of God have ever been urged to be reconciled to God, that they might partake of His blessings.

A Necessary Change

Great as is God's compassion, however, no enemy of God can expect to receive and enjoy His blessings unless a radical change takes place in his life. There is an "if" in the words of Jeremiah and unless it be taken into consideration, there is no guarantee whatever that the gifts of life enjoyed by God's covenant people will be visited upon those who have been strangers to the covenant. God hinges everything on whether the enemies become like His people, saying,

> *If they learn well the ways of my people . . . then they will be established among my people.*

That "if" demands a fundamental change in life. It was commonly known that Israel's neighbors lived lives abhorrent in the sight of God. They were idolaters, and neither recognized the Lord as their God nor worshiped Him. They profaned the Sabbath. They hated God's chosen people and attacked them without mercy when occasion offered. Their lives were immoral, stained with diverse kinds of grievous sin.

Could they be acceptable to God? Not unless they became like His people. It is sometimes forgotten that God's great requirement of men and women is that they become conformed to the image of His Son, yet that is God's aim in regeneration, the act by which He makes us *new* creatures, renewing in us His image of true knowledge, righteousness and holiness, that was lost in the fall. It is also

His purpose in sanctification, the process by which sin is lessened and holiness increased in the lives of those who have received the adoption of sonship.

Truly God's people are a peculiar people, not because of odd mannerisms and eccentricities, but because of a fundamental difference that continually shows in speech and action. It is for this reason that attention is called to the function served by Christians as letters "known and read by everybody" (2 Cor. 3:2).

Is a person at enmity with God and would he yet enjoy the blessings of His grace? Let him examine his ways. Let him check them with those of God's people, of the apostles, of Christ Himself. He should know where He stands. He cannot live just any old way and be a Christian. And if he finds little similarity between his life and the lives of God's children, let him ask of the One who is able to perform the mighty transformation necessary. That gracious Sovereign can take away the root of sin from within the soul; He can take away the fruit of sin from the life. He can bring about a revolutionary change in the one at enmity with Him, making him like God's people.

A Necessary Confession

Hand in hand with a change in life goes a change of confession. The work of God in an enemy soul does two things: It removes the enmity and it implants a firm heart belief in its place. This heart belief is like a fountain, and from it flow two streams: holiness of life and humble confession of God's grace. There is no way of stopping up the fountain so that only one of the streams will come from it.

God therefore attaches a second clause to the "if" of the text:

> If they . . . swear by my name . . . then they will be established among my people.

Israel's enemies must not only conform to the ways of God's people; they must also confess His name.

They had not done so. It was not their custom. It did not fit with their worship, nor with their lives. They had invoked the name of Baal, sworn by his name, and taught Israel to do the same. Was there great sin in this practice? The worshiper swearing by Baal declared to the world, "Baal is my God. I worship him. I serve him. I am not ashamed to own him." But he who swore by the name of the Lord, saying, "The Lord liveth," boldly asserted his faith in the Lord, the true and living God.

There had to be a reversal of practice, but the altered confession was not to be the mere recitation of vain words. Just as in the patterning of their ways after those of God's people, so here also a fundamental regenerating change in the heart itself was needed, that the confession might be a true confession.

The Necessary Concomitant

The whole situation is somewhat like Paul's description of the olive tree and branches as set forth in the eleventh chapter of Romans. Branches grafted into a good olive tree and fed by it are dominated by the nature of the tree and bring forth good fruit. The old nature is conquered and largely disappears. The testimony of the change is seen in the fruit. As the years go by, the in-grafted branches are built up together with the natural branches, are fed and nourished from the same source, and become one and the same plant structure.

In the same way enemies of God, changed in heart, are grafted into the Lord Jesus Christ. Their rebellious and sinful natures are conquered by the union, and their ways become God's ways, the ways of His people. Their confession embraces a true testimony. They are built up in spiritual life together with those who love and worship Him.

There is nothing said in the text about grace, but are we to infer that enemies become disciples in any other way than by grace? We know that God does the ingrafting, and surely that is an act of grace. We know that enmity remains enmity unless broken down by irresistible overtures of love. We know that one's confession is profane unless God-given faith rules in the heart. So let us never be deceived and think that enemies of God can become one with His people unless grace from on high works a mighty change within the soul. Outward conformity to the conduct of a Christian will never of itself guarantee a right relationship to God, either for a nation or for an individual.

As for the individual, he must become a new creature in Christ! If

God's grace has never visited him, if he does not confess the name of the Savior, if his ways are not the ways of God's people, if he is not built up with God's people so that he enjoys the blessings in which they participate, it is still possible for God's grace to take away old things and make all things new. Let him pray for that grace as it is found in the Lord Jesus, who was rich but became poor so that through His poverty those at enmity with Him might become rich (2 Cor. 8:9). Let him trust in that grace, for as Paul said to those in the Ephesian church, salvation comes by grace through faith (Eph. 2:5, 8). By grace, enemies of God become heirs of God and partake of every blessing of His covenant.

13

Jeremiah's Tears

JEREMIAH 13:15-17

Hear and pay attention,
do not be arrogant,
for the Lord has spoken.
Give glory to the Lord your God
before he brings the darkness,
before your feet stumble
on the darkening hills.
You hope for light
but he will turn it to thick darkness
and change it to deep gloom.
But if you do not listen,
I will weep in secret
because of your pride;
my eyes will weep bitterly,
overflowing with tears,
because the Lord's flock will be taken captive.

A man in tears! Some would call it a sign of weakness. Others would say, "Effeminate!" At the grave it is common; anywhere else it is rare. Yet strong men have been known to weep profusely on varied occasions. In the words of the *New England Primer,*

> Peter deny'd
> his Lord and cry'd.

Again, he in whom perfect manhood resided is recorded as being in tears three times. Small wonder, then, that a prophet of highly wrought emotional nature like Jeremiah should on occasion resort to tears.

A Portent of Destruction

There was abundant reason for crying on the part of the prophet. He had been used by God as the lone actor in a solemn drama intended to impress upon Judah the doom that awaited her. In obedience to divine instructions, he had purchased a linen belt, wrapped it about his waist, and taken care not to wash it. Subsequently he had buried the belt in a crevice in the rocks, probably by a wadi or dry riverbed near Anathoth. Then many days had passed. He had returned to the burial spot, removed the soil covering the belt, and found it rotted and useless.

A strange drama, indeed! Yet not so strange in the light of the revealed Word, for the Lord spoke and said,

> *"These wicked people . . . will be like this belt—completely useless! For as a belt is bound around a man's waist, so I bound the whole house of Israel and the whole house of Judah to me," declares the Lord, "to be my people for my renown and praise and honor. But they have not listened."*
> (Jer. 13:10, 11)

The object lesson carried out by Jeremiah was a token that the chosen people, who had lost purity and holiness by much sin and who had refused divine cleansing, were to go away into a long captivity and to be overtaken by death in a strange land in punishment for their apostasy. Sinful as his countrymen were, Jeremiah loved them and knew that the destruction they were bringing upon themselves would call forth a deep anguish in his own sympathetic heart.

A People of Apathy

So disturbed was Jeremiah as he contemplated the punishment of Judah that he wasted no time in directing to them one last appeal to repent and turn again to the God of salvation. It was a whole-souled entreaty that he made: "*Hear and* pay attention, do not be arrogant, for the Lord has spoken. Give glory to the Lord your God."

He asked no small thing. They must love what they had been accustomed to hate and hate what they had loved. Self must be crucified. They must humbly petition for forgiveness, they yielding themselves to obey God. The whole purpose of life must be reversed. Whatever they did, in word or deed, they were to do as unto the Lord.

The truth of the matter was that the people of Judah were not interested in reversing their attitude toward God. Jeremiah feared as much. They were intoxicated with both spiritual and physical lewdness. Like drunken men who wander into paths of danger without fear or concern, they would continue to disregard God's entreaties and warnings. In his heart of hearts Jeremiah knew that his plea would be in vain.

Sorrow of Soul

Even as he voiced his appeal, his heart was breaking. The tear glands of his spirit, if not of his body, had loosed their flood. He was caught amid the swirling of deep waters. Rebellion would continue, and judgment would be sure. His was a cry of anguish: "*My eyes* will weep bitterly, overflowing with tears, because the Lord's flock will be taken captive."

Can God use tears? Perhaps this incident, also, happened as an example written down as a warning (1 Cor. 10:11). Christianity would be greatly impoverished if that shortest verse of the Bible, "Jesus wept" (John 11:35), were lost or forgotten. The intercessory work of our blessed High Priest takes on new meaning when we think of the "loud cries and tears" (Heb. 5:7) that accompanied His mediatorial supplications. And what heart can remain unmoved as it envisions the Lord of Glory looking down on the city He loved, His heart filled with compassion, His eyes filled with tears?

The tears of a Christian mother have often done what her words failed to do. They have broken down the barrier and sent a sinner to the Savior. The tears of a Christian wife have sometimes proved instrumental in bringing a brute to his senses and turning him to the Lord Jesus Christ. Tears never do the work of the Word and the Spirit, but their flood often sweeps away the rocks and thorns so that the seed of the gospel may be implanted in *good* soil and bring forth fruit unto life eternal.

Jeremiah in tears! Perhaps the scoffer who mocked as Jeremiah preached was pricked in conscience by the prophet's tears, turned from his unbelief, and was saved. Men have been known to preach insincerely, but where is the man capable of shedding false tears? We may hope that Jeremiah's tears were used of God toward the salvation of souls.

Be that as it may, every Christian should pay heed to the tears of the man of Anathoth. They were tears consequent upon the revelation of God's punishment of a sinful people. They were tears of God's prophet, and God has no pleasure in the death of the wicked. His people cannot rejoice when judgment is visited upon their neighbors. Jonah had to learn this lesson. It was taught again by Jeremiah's tears. It was sealed forever as divine truth when the Son of God spoke through tears these words: "O Jerusalem, Jerusalem, you who kill the prophets and stone those sent to you, how often I have longed to gather your children together, as a hen gathers her chicks under her wings, but you were not willing" (Matt. 23:37).

Let no one think that the good news of Jesus Christ is to be communicated in a cold "take it or leave it" manner. Evangelical preaching and Christian witnessing must not be limited merely to a correct interpretation of the doctrines of the Word. We must have a love for sinners, so great a love that we will be driven urgently to unfold to them the way of salvation, whatever the cost.

Happy is he who labors in the gospel to the point of tears for the lost. Blessed is he whose compassion for the lost moves him to every effort to win them to Christ, and failing, produces not reproach but tears.

14

Three Impossible Things

JEREMIAH 13:23

Can the Ethiopian change his skin
or the leopard its spots?
Neither can you do good
who are accustomed to doing evil.

One cannot exaggerate the human interest that manifests itself on almost every page of the Bible. In just this one verse from the Book of Jeremiah is found the record of three impossible things.

The first is the inability of a black to change the color of his skin. He cannot do so. The dark pigment will not fade with washing; it does not disappear when the outer tissues are worn away with much labor. The child born of mixed racial strains who finds himself black cannot be otherwise. The black slave of the South, before the days of Lincoln, might long to be white and free, but in vain. How true it is: The skin of an Ethiopian cannot change!

A second possibility is that a leopard, that stealthy prowler of the forest, should ever become other than a spotted creature. As he is born, so must he die. Scratched by the thickets, stained with mud from the swamps, exposed to sun, wind and violent storms, the proud beast yet keeps the spots that distinguish him so well. He cannot lose them.

Would not even the sophisticated dwellers in Jerusalem listen when Jeremiah phrased a rhetorical question of so great pictorial interest? Can an Ethiopian change his skin? How absurd! They had seen one in the city just the day before. He was black as coal. Occasionally others had come to Jerusalem on commercial or political missions. They were *always* black.

Or a leopard? They had heard of this wild beast that roamed in the desolate areas south and east of the Dead Sea, along the banks of the Arnon River. They had seen skins brought into the city by traders. They could always identify them by the spots. Spots *always* belonged to a leopard!

The Related Teaching

What was the preacher driving at, anyway? His preaching had been obnoxious on other occasions. Would it be different this time? Probably not, but their curiosity was aroused and they would give ear to what he had to say.

They had not long to wait. If impossibility was the keynote of his illustrations, so was it of that which they were designed to illustrate. Jeremiah lost no time in telling them that the nation had come to the point where it could neither separate itself from sin nor perform what was good and acceptable in the sight of God. Sin had become, to all intents and purposes, a part of Judah's very nature. Her people had been taught to sin and had entered into it until sin had enslaved them and they were no longer free. It was impossible for them to do good!

So said Jeremiah. But his audience would not receive such a teaching. They did good! They treated their families well. They helped their friends. At least some of them were scrupulously honest in their business transactions. Why, they even supported the worship of the Lord and brought sacrifices to be offered at the temple! They could produce any number of witnesses who would testify to the good they performed. It was insolent of Jeremiah to pose as a prophet from God and accuse them of absolute depravity.

Jeremiah, however, was not thinking of mere kindness and justice and the fulfillment of social obligations. The "good" of which he spoke was not something external. By "good" he meant "the things of God," "things connected with salvation," "things of the Spirit," "true piety." Jeremiah was not concerned with what men regarded as good, but only with what was pleasing to God.

Now God does not commend one for being honest with his friends if he cheats his neighbors. God does not reward a man for his gifts to charity if the gifts are from ill-gotten gains. God does not approve deeds of seeming goodness on the part of one whose heart is full of pride and self-righteousness. Nor does God look with favor on him who worships in the sanctuary yet is guilty of gross immorality or is a worshiper of other gods as well. Therefore, Jeremiah spoke truly when he said, "Can the Ethiopian change his skin or the leopard its spots? Neither can you do good who are accustomed to do evil."

The Logical Application

Three impossible things: an Ethiopian changing his skin; a leopard changing its spots; the Judah of Jeremiah's day performing good in the sight of God! What does it all mean to you?

Perhaps it matters little whether one can change the color of his skin (black is beautiful!) or whether a beast can alter the figuring in its fur, but it ought to be a matter of real concern to think of a nation so habitually engaged in sin that there was no possibility of its people turning from it to do the will of God.

Too often we assume that the picture comes no closer than rebellious Pharaoh, or Jeremiah's contemporaries, or the heathen of whom Paul speaks in the first chapter of Romans. As a matter of fact, our own age has much in common with that of Jeremiah, and there are people outside the church and in it who are incapable of doing any ultimate or eternal good. They do not love God. They have no desire to obey or honor Him. God cannot recognize any relative good that may be theirs, because of the cloud of their sin, which blots it from His view.

As sin more and more dominates an individual or a group, there is less and less possibility of a change toward righteousness. Sin is a hard master. Its wages look attractive at first, but sooner or later utter slavery is demanded—slavery from which the victims are unable to escape.

Consider how prone we all are to sin. Satan would give us no peace. Who has not cried out with Paul, "Who will rescue me from this body of death" (Rom. 7:24)? Surely we have felt our own inability to bring about the necessary transformation.

Thank God, some have found that what is impossible with man is possible with God, and that "if anyone is in Christ, he is a new creation" (2 Cor. 5:17). He who has been born again knows that the work of God in his soul not only prevents him from sinking to the helpless level of the Jews whom Jeremiah addressed but also, in spite of his shortcomings, enables him to do what God regards as good.

If one has never experienced the regenerating power of God, let him be admonished by Jeremiah's words as to his sick and helpless condition of sin. He can no more save himself than an Ethiopian can change his skin. But he can ask the Great Physician for cleansing of heart and healing of soul. God is a God of unlimited power and exceeding great grace.

Have you already found victory over sin through the Lord Jesus Christ? If so, may the "three impossible things" remind you of the sovereign grace that took you out of the pit, and may you abound in thanksgiving and praise to the God of deliverance.

15

Wandering Jews
—and Gentiles

JEREMIAH 14:10

This is what the Lord says about this people:
They greatly love to wander;
  they do not restrain their feet.
So the Lord does not accept them;
  he will now remember their wickedness
and punish them for their sins.

According to the legend of the Wandering Jew, our Lord paused before the door of Joannes Buttadeus while on His way to Calvary. The Jew, however, drove Him away, saying, "Go! Why dost thou tarry?" But Jesus, looking sternly at him, rebuked him with these words, "I go, but thou shalt tarry 'til I come." Though he repented and became a changed man, Joannes Buttadeus could not die, and in the succeeding centuries he wandered from place to place throughout the earth.

The legend of the wandering Jew arose from the confusing of certain incidents mentioned in the Bible. Historically, it is untrue. Yet strangely enough the Bible does speak of wandering Jews, for in our text is recorded a description of the people of Judah in Jeremiah's time.

There is probably no more apt characterization of them than this: "They greatly love to wander." Their first and dominating love was not for their Lord but for wandering from Him. The word used by Jeremiah is not one primarily descriptive of mere moving from one place to another. It indicates the staggering course of the drunkard and the unsteady gait of mariners as their ship is tossed by an angry storm. Describing the faint and uncertain tottering of the beggar, it also pictures the unstable ways of the harlot. It is ideally applied to men seeking to escape the controlling hand of God that they may enter unrestrained upon a course of sin. Jeremiah so employs it.

Where It Began

As a matter of fact, almost all biblical mentions of wandering are either actual departures from God or have some intimate connection with turning away from Him. It was because Cain killed his brother that he became a wanderer on the face of the earth. The sin of unbelief was responsible for the years of wilderness wandering on the part of the Israelites. Isaiah was thinking of the universality of sin when he said, "We all, like sheep, have gone astray" (Isa. 53:6). And the Good Shepherd spoke not of a lamb absent from its Palestinian sheepfold but of one wandering away from God when He told of the ninety and nine (Luke 15:4).

Read the Old Testament Scriptures. Their testimony is unanimous—the Jews were a people constantly straying from God. Condense the Bible witness to a single statement, and this is the result: Wandering from God was their first love.

All of Us Wander

Wandering Jews! We find it easy to reproach them, but is not the same true of us? Do we not love to wander, too? The human race, fallen with its first representative, is a wandering people. It was for this that Christ must come, that He might seek out and save the lost. And he who is not rescued by the Good Shepherd remains lost and continues in his wandering.

This is the song of the Christian:

> I was a wandering sheep,
> I did not love the fold;
> I did not love my Shepherd's voice,
> I would not be controlled.

Our first love was for wandering, but God put a new love in our hearts, a love for obedience, a love for Him.

It is so natural for a vagabond to think that his wanderings are unobserved, but God sees all that he does and knows all the places he goes. No less does He mark the course of the spiritual vagabond. And while He *forgets* the sins of the penitent, He *remembers* the iniquities of the wanderer. This was His declaration to Judah through Jeremiah.

Not only is God aware of the sins of the wanderer, but those sins separate him from God. Moses, David, Hezekiah, Josiah, the prophets and every righteous, believing Jew had sweet communion with God, but Jeremiah's contemporaries had lost that fellowship. Jeremiah told them that it was because of their wandering, because of their sin. Like the psalmist, he knew that only those with clean hands and pure hearts are acceptable before the Lord (Psa. 24:4).

His message was not ended, however. The justice of God demanded that the wanderer suffer just punishment for his sin, and so he went on to say that God would "punish them for their sins." The divine covenant promised blessing to an obedient people but made plain the fact that wanderers would bring on themselves curse after curse.

How true were the words of the covenant! How wandering Jews have suffered throughout the years! They have become outcasts, natural branches broken from the tree, unacceptable to God. Their punishment has seemed almost greater than a people could bear. Persecuted, reviled, exiled, slaughtered—they have reaped a just reward for their sins. And all the time God has extended to them the offer of full and free reconciliation and salvation through the

Messiah, whom they rejected and put to death. Wandering Jews, O that you might become repentant like Joannes Buttadeus!

But wandering Gentiles, there is no more hope for you unless you also forsake your wandering and embrace the Son of God as your Savior, Example and Guide. Wander no more! Make this your confession of penitence:

> I've wandered far away from God,
> Now I'm coming home;
> The paths of sin too long I've trod,
> Lord, I'm coming home.
>
> Coming home, coming home,
> Nevermore to roam,
> Open wide Thine arms of love,
> Lord, I'm coming home.

16

Words Sweet and Bitter

JEREMIAH 15:16

When your words came, I ate them;
* they were my joy and my heart's delight,*
for I bear your name,
* O Lord God Almighty.*

Psalm 119:103 reads: "How sweet are your words to my taste, sweeter than honey to my mouth." What a beautiful description of divine revelation! One contemplates the majestic glory of his Maker, whose throne is heaven, whose footstool is the earth, before whom the cherubim hide their faces and lift aloud their voices in adoration, saying, "Holy, holy, holy is the Lord Almighty; the whole earth is full of his glory" (Isa. 6:3). He thinks of God's plan of salvation through the substitutionary atonement of Christ, the knowledge that God loved us and gave Himself for us. He meditates on the matchless love, the amazing grace and the unbounded mercy which found expression in the Savior's humiliation and suffering that sinners might be restored to fellowship with God. He remembers the promises of God, which are ever faithful and true, more precious than fine stones or silver or gold. Yes, the words of the living God are sweet beyond measure.

The Bitter

Perhaps the Psalmist had in mind only one aspect of God's revelation. It would be strange if God's word to men were unmixed sweetness. Consider life. The bitter is strangely mingled with the sweet. Joy is tempered by sorrow. Victory is often but a prelude to final, catastrophic defeat. Even the Christian knows conflict within and is sometimes led to exclaim, "What I do is not the good I want to do; no, the evil I do not want to do—this I keep on doing" (Rom. 7:19).

The root of bitterness is sin, and so long as sin continues it will produce what is bitter. And because God's word to us is especially concerned with sin, its heinousness in His sight and its awful dominion over us, it must surely be expected that here, also, the bitter will accompany the sweet.

Jeremiah found it so. Moreover, his prophetic messages were not to a faithful congregation but to an apostate people. Lacking in good tidings, they were filled with condemnation. Like Amos, Jeremiah was a prophet of judgment. His task was not an easy one. It was not pleasant to have to prophesy the doom of his own nation. There was no joy in acquainting his fellowmen with a knowledge of the coming captivity and the terrible punishments to be visited on them for their sins.

With a feeling of timidity and an aching heart, the prophet addressed the people. Sometimes the performance of his commission was almost more than he could bear. If only he could have been the pastor of an obedient flock! But no, the word of God that he must speak was bitter beyond compare.

When God came to dwell among men, not all of His words were of comfort and tranquility. Many of them were words of judgment against unrighteousness. In Matthew Jesus said: "I did not come to bring peace, but a sword" (10:34). "Woe to the world because of the things that cause people to sin!" (18:7) "The kingdom of God will be taken away from you" (21:43). "Woe to you, teachers of the law and

Pharisees, you hypocrites!" (23:13). "They will go away to eternal punishment" (25:46).

Some of His words were prophetic of trouble and hardship for believers: "If they persecuted me, they will persecute you also" (John 15:20). "You will be handed over to be persecuted and put to death, and you will be hated by all nations because of me" (Matt. 24:9).

Bitter words, these!

The divine message is not of a different nature today. The faithful Christian witness must declare God's judgment against sin. We must publish the fact that the one who rejects Christ and refuses to repent is lost. We must make it plain that "Whoever does not believe stands condemned already because he has not believed in the name of God's one and only Son" (John 3:18). Yes, God's hard sayings are not easy to proclaim.

The Sweet

In the face of all this, how surprising to turn to the Book of Jeremiah and consider the prophet's testimony regarding the prophetic messages he had received from God: "When your words came, I ate them; they were my joy and my heart's delight." Nor was he thinking of the brighter side of God's revelation. Rather, as the following verse shows, he spoke of the woes God had pronounced through him upon Judah. Why such a witness? Why was it not like that of John in his vision on the Isle of Patmos? For the scroll of condemnatory prophecy was for John sweet only to the taste and exceedingly bitter afterward.

Perhaps the answer is to be found in the common experiences of life. Bitter as it is sometimes, we welcome the medicine that promises to make us well. On occasion the performance of a disagreeable task is rendered joyous, either as one considers the end or thinks of the one for whom it is being done. Again, it may be that a person receives satisfaction, knowing that he is doing what it is his duty to do. Truly, there are many things able to make sweet that which is bitter.

The secret of Jeremiah's witness is to be found in the words that follow those quoted above: "For I bear your name, O Lord God Almighty." Jeremiah knew God. He worshiped and loved Him. He had learned that man does not live by bread alone but by every word that comes from the mouth of God. Like Enoch, he walked with God. Moreover, God had chosen him as a special vessel to make known his will to men, and the office of a prophet was glorious, indeed. Therefore, bitter or sweet, hard or gentle, understood or veiled in mystery, the words of God were to Jeremiah true, enduring and of pure delight. They burned like a fire within him, and as Paul later cried, "Woe to me if I do not preach the gospel!" (1 Cor. 9:16). So Jeremiah might have spoken of the impelling constraint that the words of God placed on him. However unpleasant it might be to declare them, they were the words of God, therefore wonderful words, precious and sweet to Jeremiah, who thought only of the One who spoke them.

Are there hard sayings in the Scriptures? Do not be rebellious. Do not fear. Do not sorrow. The God who has spoken through the inspired writings is the same God who works all things after the counsel of His own will. And He is a God of truth and love! Whatever God does is surely good. He knows best. His chastisement is both wise and necessary.

But as in the case of Jeremiah the bitter can be made sweet only if the God of heaven is *your* God. If He is your God, the bitterness is removed from His words. His judgment against sin will not come near you, for there is no condemnation to those who are in Christ Jesus. Persecution and tribulation may be your lot, but the Lord has sent the Comforter to dwell in your heart. For you, what is bitter becomes sweet.

May you trust in Jeremiah's God.

17

Depending on the Flesh
JEREMIAH 17:5, 6

This is what the Lord says:
Cursed is the one who trusts in man,
   who depends on flesh for his strength
   and whose heart turns away from the Lord.
He will be like a bush in the wastelands;
   he will not see prosperity when it comes.
He will dwell in the parched places of the desert,
   in a salt land where no one lives.

A t the close of a sermon preached during the great Philadelphia revival of 1858 the Rev. George Duffield, in lines of his own composition, exhorted his people:

> Stand up!—stand up for Jesus!
> Stand in his strength alone;
> The arm of flesh will fail you—
> Ye dare not trust your own.

Perhaps he was thinking of his young friend who, the Sunday before, had preached in the power of the Spirit as a great company of men and women were saved. That young man's life was suddenly snatched away a few days later when his sleeve became caught in a machine and his arm was torn out by the roots. Be that as it may, I should like to think that the words of the prophet Jeremiah were ringing in his heart: "*Cursed is* the one who trusts in man, who depends on flesh for his strength."

Where Is Our Reliance?

Jeremiah's words speak first of all about the individual who depends on human resources rather than on the Lord of heaven and earth, but they are preceded by a context in which a nation is threatened by war and destruction. The words are applicable not just to individuals but to nations as well.

His words ought to ring in our ears, not by themselves but in their context, for the following verse of Scripture describes the pitiful state of one who depends on the flesh. When faced with threats of war, we might say to aggressors, "The arm of flesh will fail you." But would our words accomplish more than those of a fanatic who once made it his practice to cable or telephone warlike powers threatening our nation?

It would be better for us to urge this truth upon our own leaders. Just possibly they would listen, and they would listen if the church of Jesus Christ in our country would itself believe the same truth enough to do something about it.

Again, we might wisely apply the truth to our own hearts. We blandly talk of trusting God, but in the last analysis do we not depend on the flesh? The fact that our cause may be right does not excuse us. God says, "Cursed is the one who . . . depends on flesh." We need what we do not have: perfect, abiding trust in God, not only in national crises but also in our churches and in our homes.

In 1858, when Dudley Tyng preached his dying message in Jaynes' Hall, the clouds of civil war were on the horizon. Yet an estimated fifth of his vast audience of 5,000 that day responded by pledging themselves not to depend on flesh but to put their trust in the King of Glory.

When threats of war confront us, or we hear the clash of resounding arms, the plea to trust in God rather than in earthly powers always seems to fall on deaf ears. Instead, there is reliance on increased taxes, armaments, plans for defense. Not only do we neglect to put our trust in God—we rob Him! The day of rest, God's day, was instituted by Him as a day of prayer; then it becomes but another day for the wheels of war industries to grind feverishly. Our time, our money, our lives, our hopes—they all depend on the flesh. Would that God might help us to do something about it when war's dangers appear at our doors.

Where Is Our Trust?

In wartime a Canadian pastor wrote of the town in which he was ministering, "People think they are the salt of the earth but are the worst of proud, haughty, self-centered sinners. We surely need an awakening . . . and unless we get it throughout the empire we shall lose the war."

One cannot help but like the ring of this man's words. They sound as though he sincerely believed that unless his people forsook the arm of flesh and really trusted in God, they would lose the war. His were not mere pious phrases. O that we, too, might gain such conviction!

Do I hear someone saying, "What about Christian Netherlands in World War II? She trusted God rather than arms. Would she not better have depended on the flesh?" However, not all the people of the Netherlands were Christians and, in any case,we should be slow to question either the sovereignty or love of God. The hymnist makes this commentary on plights of the faithful, but the words are relevant to nations as well as to individuals:

> When through fiery trials thy pathway shall lie,
> My grace, all-sufficient, shall be thy supply;
> The flame shall not hurt thee; I only design
> Thy dross to consume, and thy gold to refine.
>
> The soul that on Jesus hath leaned for repose,
> I will not—I will not desert to his foes;
> That soul—though all hell should endeavor to shake,
> I'll never—no never—no never forsake!

This is a security of which the world knows nothing. It depends on no earthly might, no human power, no man-made armaments. It is rooted in the omnipotence of the Almighty and is as sure as His promises. The strongest battalions of evil are powerless to overthrow it.

Though dependence on the flesh may show itself in the form of conquering legions, the curse of God rests upon it. At such a time, trust in God may seem a pitiful defense, but God will ever be the all-satisfying portion of His people.

Beyond Understanding

A party of explorers makes its way through the desert. The sands are hot and burning. The glare from the desert floor is so intense that it blinds unprotected eyes. No green plant is in sight. Water is a foreign substance. Suddenly a member of the party cries out. He points. The others follow his finger. There in the distance is something or somebody. It almost seems like the figure of a man. They draw closer. It *is!* But what a sad specimen of humanity! The man is in tatters. He is emaciated. His eyes sunken, he stares uncertainly about him, seeming to recognize their approach. He is a derelict of the desert. His speech is unintelligible. Though alive, he is as dead. The words of cheer from his rescuers mean nothing to him. His senses no longer serve him. His understanding is gone.

Such is God's description of the man who depends on the flesh. He is cut off from the enjoyment of life. His growth stunted, he lives in a place of narrow horizons. "He will not see prosperity when it comes." A noted preacher once suggested his plight in these words: "God comes, and I would rather have some more money. God comes, and I prefer some woman's love. God comes, and I would rather have a prosperous business. God comes, and I prefer beer."

I sometimes think of the aggressors as they plot wars of conquest. I wonder what life can ever hold for them, whether in victory or defeat. What is good has no power to satiate their appetites. They delight only in lust, greed, power, blood. They depend on the flesh only to become like the victim of the desert, insensible to all that is good. How terrible is the state of such a man!

Examples of Irreligion

But let us come closer home. Let us think of that little Canadian community where even the church people were self-righteous and proud. There is no wall between Maine and the Maritimes, with one kind of people on one side and another kind on the other. If the trust of these, our neighbors, is mostly on the surface rather than in the heart, should we not be honest and admit the same of ourselves?

An Iowa farmer was irreligious but frank when he refused to say grace before meals, contending, "I see no need for offering thanks for my meals; I work for what I get." Yet there are many of us who make a show of righteousness but in our heart of hearts trust no more in God than did this foolish man who openly proclaimed entire dependence on the flesh.

Just how fully do you trust God? Is it mainly a surface trust? Even Hitler and Mussolini expressed confidence that God would vindicate their course, as though they rested faith in Him. Do you pray before setting your hand to each task, large or small? When did you last make confession before God of your sinfulness and weakness and need of strength from above? How often do you *pray* rather than *recite* the Lord's Prayer? If required to choose between a bomb shelter and the watch-care of God, which would you actually choose?

Dependence on the flesh failed the Iowa farmer; illness overtook him and made him unable to work. Sooner or later, it fails everyone. The only alternative is to trust in God and in His gift of love, the person of His Son, the Lord Jesus Christ. To trust in Him is to put on the gospel armor. Then, watching unto prayer, we may rest secure in every storm, and at last, with the King of Glory, reign eternally.

18

The Untrustworthy Heart
JEREMIAH 17:9

*The heart is deceitful above all things
and beyond cure.
Who can understand it?*

Who trusts the word of tyrants? Who dares trust the changing policies of many of the world's nations? How far does labor trust capital? Do the various organizations of a community trust one another? Do you leave your house unlocked and trust passersby? What of your friends? Do you fully trust them? And is your trust in other members of your family as complete as it might be? Be honest! Is not your attitude toward other groups and individuals largely one of question, or suspicion, or distrust, or reservation? Do you not hold back the fullest measure of trust and avoid placing it in those about you? Unhappy experience has pointed us toward such a policy.

The result is that we reserve complete trust for ourselves. We trust our own hearts. We rest assured that our own wills and minds are alone worthy of our fullest confidence. We feel most secure when our secrets are not divulged and our purposes are locked deep within our hearts. We then fear no betrayal. We do not doubt but that our own best interests will be served.

A Deceitful Companion

We are wrong! Perhaps we cannot trust those about us; neither can we trust our own hearts! The God-given picture of those hearts is this:

> *The heart is deceitful above all things*
> *and beyond cure.*

It is a deceitful companion. You must not trust it. Since the fall of our first parents, the human heart, left to itself, has manifested only corruption and depravity. The prophet has characterized it as incurably sick. Moreover, he has described it as treacherous. It would be only folly to trust in such a heart.

In what does the deceit lie? Our Lord gave the answer when He said, "Out of the heart come evil thoughts, murder, adultery, sexual immorality, theft, false testimony, slander" (Matt. 15:19). The natural heart gives birth to all these things, and they defile us. They constitute lawlessness in the sight of God. They reap for us civil punishment, social ostracism and physical suffering. The heart, desperately wicked and deceitful above all things, tempts people with the prospect of delight in evil deeds and denies that they will eventually bring unhappiness. Is not such a heart a deceitful and untrustworthy companion?

"O yes," replies the average unbeliever, "but my heart isn't like that. I don't do such things." Where, however, does he find such an answer? His own deceitful heart gives it to him. The teaching of the Lord Jesus does not give one such assurance. It awakens him to the fact that the social sins Jesus mentioned are only the beginning of sins, and that the universal traits of pride and self-righteousness betray the utter corruption of men's hearts. Therefore, if the non-Christian defends his own righteousness, he puts himself in the class of the Pharisee who made of public prayer an opportunity for boasting. And everyone knows Christ's judgment concerning the Pharisee's heart. It was no less condemnatory than Jeremiah's words: "*The heart* is deceitful above all things and beyond cure."

Another prophet once spoke words that are to the point here. He said, "We all, like sheep, have gone astray" (Isa. 53:6). Likewise, a noted apostle declared, "All have turned away . . . there is no one who does good" (Rom. 3:12). What made us all go astray? What made us all sin? There is only one answer—the untrustworthy heart.

I venture to suggest that in all the world there is no sin of more disastrous consequences than the sin of wandering away from God, regardless of what form that sin may take. You do not have to become a drunkard in order to reject your Maker and turn from Him. Live to yourself and withhold from Him the worship and honor that are His due, and you automatically exclude yourself from the kingdom of heaven. No greater tragedy can come to a human soul, and yet it is the heart of deceit that people are prone to trust.

I wonder what you would do if you had a friend who led you into a life of drunkenness and accompanying degradation. What if such a one who used his influence to teach you to gamble and to make you lose all your money, and made you his companion in thievery until you were caught and punished? The human heart is such a friend. It is a deceitful companion. Can you possibly trust it?

The Divine Prescription

Perhaps we would be completely deceived by our hearts if God had not told us of their true character, but could words be plainer than these? "*The heart* is deceitful above all things and beyond cure." God says that we need new hearts, regenerate hearts, hearts that will give birth to love for Him and our fellowmen. We need hearts that will be humble and prone to worship our wonderful King, hearts that will counsel us to flee from sin and all unrighteousness. The natural heart is stony; we need hearts of flesh. The natural heart is deceitful; we need honest, sincere hearts. The natural heart is desperately wicked; we need pure, holy hearts.

Only the Divine Surgeon can perform the operation that will give us such hearts as are necessary. We cannot barter for them in the markets of the world. We cannot make them. They are a creation of God.

Let no one be satisfied until he has a trustworthy heart. Let him not rest until such a heart is his. Rather, let him look upon his natural heart with suspicion and distrust, and ever pray for God's gift of a holy heart.

You say that you have a trustworthy heart? If so, continue to pray that the God who gave it will give it dominion and mastery over your whole life. Daily ask Him to cleanse it from any defilement of sin. Make it the object of special prayer from time to time. And never forget to give thanks to the eternal, loving God for taking away that corrupt heart of deceit and wickedness.

19

At Jerusalem's Gates

JEREMIAH 17:20-27

There is something fascinating about the picture of an ancient Oriental city with its heavy walls and solid, massive gates. Such gates were once the defense of the city. At night or in times of danger they were closed, and invaders were kept from entering. By day they were open, and busy figures thronged in and out of the city. Business of all kinds was transacted beneath their shadows. Justice was meted out nearby. The gates of Jerusalem were like that.

The Old Testament Sabbath

One day a prophet stood in the gate through which kings and commoners were accustomed to pass. A crowd began to gather about him. The bargaining of tradesmen was interrupted for the moment. There was a noticeable hush about the gateway. The prophet was about to speak.

He began as one with authority:

> *Hear the word of the Lord, O kings of Judah and all people of Judah and everyone living in Jerusalem who come through these gates. This is what the Lord says: Be careful not to carry a load on the Sabbath day or bring it through the gates of Jerusalem. Do not bring a load out of your houses or do any work on the Sabbath, but keep the Sabbath day holy, as I commanded your forefathers. Yet they did not listen or pay attention; they were stiff-necked and would not listen or respond to discipline. But if you are careful to obey me, declares the Lord, and bring no load through the gates of this city on the Sabbath, but keep the Sabbath day holy by not doing any work on it, then kings who sit on David's throne will come through the gates of this city with their officials. They and their officials will come riding in chariots and on horses, accompanied by the men of Judah and those living in Jerusalem, and this city will be inhabited forever. . .*
>
> *But if you do not obey me to keep the Sabbath day holy by not carrying any load as you come through the gates of Jerusalem on the Sabbath day, then I will kindle an unquenchable fire in the gates of Jerusalem that will consume her fortresses.*

Then the prophet went on to the next gate. There he repeated the performance, and so on from gate to gate until all had been visited.

Jeremiah, the prophet at Jerusalem's gates, told the people that their government, the royal line of David, and the city itself would be forever secure if only they would respect the Sabbath and keep it holy. Through those very gates Davidic kings and princes would ever continue to pass. The glory of Jerusalem would remain undimmed; its independence and safety would be assured, but the Sabbath must be kept!

Further, the prophet told his Jerusalem audiences that proper observance of the Sabbath would lead to the prosperity of the lawful worship of their covenant God. If they were faithful in this respect, worshipers from the surrounding hamlets and countryside would stream through Jerusalem's gates with gifts for the temple and its services. The implication was that their neglect of the Sabbath ordinance would lead to the disintegration of the kingdom program.

God's threat of doom upon a Sabbath-breaking people brought the prophet's message to a close. Those who thronged the gates might disregard the prophetic warning, but unless they should repent and keep the Lord's day holy, the God of judgment would cause those very gates to be destroyed by fire.

They did not heed his words. A few years went by, and the marauding soldiers of a conquering host razed Jerusalem's walls and burned her gates. For long years the gates lay in ruin. Almost a century and a half passed. Then one night a dark figure emerged from the ruined city of Zion by way of the Valley Gate, made his way to the Dung Gate, from there to the Gate of the Fountain, and back by the way he had come. Everywhere he observed how the gates had been consumed by fire.

Nor did he doubt but that God had been true to His word as threatened by Jeremiah. The man's name was Nehemiah. He believed God and feared that his condemnation might again be visited on the Sabbath-breakers of Jerusalem. Like Abraham Lincoln, when opportunity came to strike against an evil, he did so with all the energy and determination at his command. As you may read in the last chapter of his memoirs, the sanctity of the Sabbath was most carefully preserved while he remained in authority. Truly he was a man of God.

The Sabbath Today

Today no walls hem in our cities and villages. Normally we have no city gates like those of old. Instead, great streams of people enter along dozens of traffic arteries. Yet on all these busy avenues one looks in vain for a prophet with a like message. There are thousands of billboards but not one has any such suggestion. Car radios bring notice after notice to motorists as they stream along with the traffic—announcements concerning the Sabbath—but they are of ball games, movies, rodeos, golf tournaments, fishing, hunting and picnic opportunities. Newsboys pass between the lines of cars with the latest editions of the city papers, but no Sabbath proclamation is in them.

In fact, little is said in the churches about a Christian's responsibility for keeping the Sabbath Day holy, and sincere Christians raise the question of whether under the New Covenant there is any Sabbath-keeping requirement. Those who contend that there is no such requirement argue that the Sabbath commandment was part and parcel of the ceremonial laws of Old Testament times, along with other prescribed days of rest and animal sacrifices. They say that the Sabbath was but a part of the theocratic arrangement by which God and His servants ruled the Jewish kingdom, and that the theocracy is a thing of the past. They point out that cities cannot be expected to screen the traffic entering them on the Sabbath Day or to take other measures to shut down businesses on that day. Sunday "Blue Laws" have been repealed.

They consider the command relevant for the simple agricultural life of the Jewish people in ancient times. But, they contend, the complex life of modern times does not at all adapt itself to such a pattern of life. God's demands on the Christian are in spiritual and moral realms, they insist, rather than in external observances.

They claim that if we insist on Sabbath observance we should also enforce the Old Testament penalty for Sabbath-breaking—stoning the offender to death.

To complicate the situation further, some call attention to the fact that Christians who accept responsibility for keeping the Sabbath ought to observe the seventh rather than the first day of the week. They challenge the validity of switching the day of worship, as the early Christians did, to a day other than that prescribed by Moses.

One hears other voices, however. They observe that the Sabbath commandment is embedded in God's great moral law, the Ten Commandments. It is therefore to be differentiated from the other sabbaths found in the ceremonial law. They indicate that the expressed purpose of the Sabbath was twofold. It was to be a reminder of how in creation God performed the creative acts for six days but rested on the seventh. It was also a further reminder of the wonderful grace of God in bringing His people out of a land of slavery into a land of freedom and blessing. Although the regulations of the ceremonial law were fulfilled with the mediatorial work of Christ and were therefore without further purpose, the keeping of the Sabbath or the Lord's Day has a timeless purpose.

And it is the judgment of most of Christendom that there is

justified continuity between the Sabbath of the Old Covenant and the Lord's Day of the covenant that followed.

If the Sabbath was recognized in the days of the prophets as "the Lord's holy day" (Isa. 58:13) and if our Savior is indeed "Lord of the Sabbath" (Matt. 12:8), we ought to think twice before looking on it as our own day, a day no different from other days.

Does the Sabbath not commend itself as a remarkable provision of God that there should be a pause in the tempo of life, one day in seven to give us a special day set aside for worship and for the refreshing of our bodies, a "day of joy and gladness"? Does not history verify the fact that Sabbath observance has been a great blessing wherever it has been practiced?

Quite apart from *obligation*, doesn't the Christian find rich reward in pausing on Resurrection Day each week to honor his Lord in a special way? Surely the Christian attitude toward that day should be first of all not a day of negative connotations but, as for Isaiah, a day of delight, honoring the Lord. If the Sabbath was a legal requirement under Old Testament law, who will say that with our Christian liberty we should not go *beyond* what the saints of old were obliged to do?

One day a youth was peddling fresh farm vegetables from door to door. When one door opened, a little man with a black headpiece declined to make a purchase, saying, "It is *the day*!" Ought we to be less conscious of the special character of the *Lord's* Day?

Regardless of whether we think of the keeping of the Lord's Day as a *requirement*, we can be sure of this: If we use it for communion with God (both privately and with God's people), for rest for our bodies, for doing good to others, and for witnessing to the lost, the God of Heaven will be well-pleased.

20

The Potter and the Clay
JEREMIAH 18:1-10

The clay banks alongside a mid-western road once furnished the material from which the children of a near-by farmhouse were accustomed to fashion marbles, candlesticks and utensils of various kinds and descriptions. Small hands would mold the clay into the desired shapes. It would then be baked to brittle hardness in the oven of the farmhouse kitchen range.

Child thoughts would occupy the minds of the little potters as they worked with the clay, and it is safe to say that they were quite ignorant of the fact that the eternal God in his holy Word had recorded truth that had much to do with the labor in which they were engaged.

In Scripture we are told that the prophet Jeremiah, in obedience to God's command, once visited the workshop of a professional worker in clay. He watched intently as with deft movements the potter fashioned a vessel on his wheel, noted an imperfection, crumpled the marred vessel into an unformed mass, and worked it again on the wheel until its beauty and perfection quite satisfied his exacting standards.

The Sovereign Craftsman

Jeremiah was doubtless fascinated by all that he observed, but it was not God's purpose merely to provide for his entertainment. God wanted him to view the proceeding with homiletic eyes and to use it as a potent illustration of the sovereign power of the Lord God over earthly kingdoms—and if over the kingdoms of men, then over every individual within those kingdoms and also over every lesser kingdom of creation. The kingdom of Judah might vaunt itself proudly, but the heaven-drawn picture of it was this—*clay in the hands of the Potter.*

Ours would be a different world if men in general believed absolutely that God is almighty. If this truth ruled men's hearts, they would greatly fear to incur His wrath, would present themselves humbly before Him, and would tremble for fear they might offend against His perfect righteousness.

Many of us give verbal assent to the omnipotence of God but never feel the least constraint to make our lives conform to that belief. Is it not because we have never received the teaching into our hearts and given it loving acceptance as divine truth? Would that each of us might, even now, believe with our whole heart that our own life and every life and the life of every nation are in God's hands as clay in the hands of a potter!

With this clay the Great Potter works. He fashions some vessels unto honor and some unto dishonor, according to the secret counsel of His own will. No mere creature has the right to question the wisdom or righteousness of what He sovereignly performs, not even the vessel of wrath. It is enough to know that He is omniscient, allwise, altogether good. His Word so declares. Trust that it is so!

Responsible Creatures

There is one important difference between men and clay. Clay is a lifeless substance. It is entirely passive in the potter's hands. Men and women are the crown of God's creation, endued with life, and possessing wills of their own. They know the difference between right and wrong and have the capability to make moral choices. The Potter's hand on them is sovereign but never shapes them contrary to their own will. Entire responsibility for their actions and for their final end is laid upon them.

When Jeremiah declared to Judah that she was but clay in the Potter's hands, could Judah fold her hands and disclaim responsibility for her sinful course? Could she blame God for her failures and iniquities? A thousand times, No! So that not only one side of the truth be presented by the illustration of the potter, God directed His prophet to make clear the fact that divinely revealed decrees of either blessing or punishment are always contingent on human conduct. Let the heirs of God's promises sin, and His wrath will be visited upon them—they will be cut off from His mercy. Let transgressors repent in sincerity before the Lord, and they will receive life and inherit every other benefit of the covenant of grace.

We follow a false and defenseless course if we live in defiance of the truth that God is the Potter and we the clay, but just as defenseless is our alibi if we try to excuse our actions on the ground that it is God who works in us and shapes our destiny without our being responsible. On the day of Pentecost did not Peter declare it was the Potter's predetermined plan that His beloved Son should be taken by men and crucified on the cross? Yet Peter just as clearly singled out the perpetrators of this crime as "wicked" men and so responsible to the God of judgment for their terrible sin of hanging Him on the tree!

The Potter is able to punish; He is also able to bless. He will punish us if we in any way turn aside from obeying His commands and refuse to repent and seek His help to mend our ways. He will bless us if we walk with Him and do His will, and, with godly sorrow for our disobedience, humbly confess our past sins. Can I then do other than make this my prayer?

Have Thine own way, Lord!
    Have Thine own way!
Thou art the Potter;
    I am the clay.
Mould me and make me
    After Thy will,
While I am waiting,
    Yielded and still.

Have Thine own way, Lord!
    Have Thine own way!
Hold o'er my being
    Absolute sway!
Fill with Thy Spirit
    Till all shall see
Christ only, always,
    Living in me!

21

The Fate of an Unjust King
JEREMIAH 22:13-19

In the imagination of children, kings belong to the realm of fable and legend and have no share in the everyday world in which we live. More mature youth, given to hero worship, picture the royal personage as the grandest being on earth and covet the privilege of some day actually seeing a king in all his splendor. The coronation ceremony is always proof of yet another truth—the fancies and dreams of childhood, though often imprisoned and secret, still dominate adult emotions, and men with gray hair and bowed frames are thrilled at the sight of the king in all his resplendent pomp and glory.

It is difficult for us to realize that kings are human, that they undergo the same experiences which come to us. They are tempted, they sin, and they are visited by divine judgment. Yet this is all true—too true, sometimes—and the Bible gives many such instances that we may be admonished to flee from similar sins.

Serious Charges

One of the last kings of Judah was a man of wicked character. Originally his name was Eliakim, but he bought from the powerful ruler of Egypt the right to rule and was given by this pharaoh a new name, Jehoiakim.

To Jehoiakim, the throne of Judah signified nothing of responsibility, either to God, that he should walk in the fear of the Lord, or to his subjects, that he should consider their welfare and reign in justice and with mercy. Mercilessly, Jehoiakim exacted from the people the price Pharaoh Necho had demanded for the throne.

He also impressed them into his service and, without wages, compelled them to erect regal palaces that would vie in splendor with those of Ahab and Solomon. His father, the godly Josiah, had trembled at the recitation of God's requirements as written in Scripture, but his hardened son plunged a penknife into the scroll of Jeremiah's prophecy and threw it angrily into the fire. The woes pronounced by another prophet kindled his wrath to such an extent that he sought this prophet's life, dispatched unprincipled men to seize him as he fled into Egypt, and with his own sword ended the life of the man of God. The worship of Assyrian deities flourished in Judah, and no effort was made to bring about a purity of religion. Jehoiakim had no concern for the religion of almighty God. Of some men the Bible says nothing bad; of this man it says nothing good.

Moreover, God was to bring him face to face with his sins, condemn them in no uncertain terms, and warn him that unless he changed his ways he would bring utter ruin upon himself and the nation. In accordance with God's purpose, the prophet Jeremiah went down one day from the temple to the royal palace and boldly charged the king with his various sins: violence, oppression, undue love of money and luxurious display, vanity, injustice, bloodshed. The charges were pointed and stinging. Without doubt, embarrassment and rage must have seized the proud sovereign, and from that day we may be sure that he was a sworn enemy of Jeremiah. But Jeremiah had been faithful to his Lord's command and had done only what God had directed him to do.

Grave Consequences

Before his message to Jehoiakim was finished, he prophesied the king's fate if he refused to repent. Like the "man without a country," he would come to the end of life "unwept, unhonored, and unsung." No royal procession would bear him to the grave. No mourners would lift their voices in lamentation. His dead body would be thrown outside the city into the open field where the birds of heaven could swoop down and devour it. No one would care. As Eliphas the Temanite appropriately remarked, "Those who plow evil and those who sow trouble reap it" (Job 4:8).

Just how the prophecy was fulfilled we do not know. The writers of Scripture barely mention his death. The historian Josephus says that Nebuchadnezzar killed him and threw his body outside the city walls, unburied. We can well believe this to be true. For eleven years he played the unfeeling despot and defied heaven and earth. For eleven years he ground the poor beneath his heel. For eleven years he sneered at justice. But when the eleven years had come to their full, the tables were turned and justice emerged the victor. God was still on His throne!

Timely Observations

What does life mean to us, anyway? Are we like Jehoiakim? Are we merely interested in making our mark in the world? Are we out to seize what we can and "let the devil take the hindmost"? The world is full of such people today. Or do we feel compassion toward the poor? Do we try to share the burdens of those who are helpless and unfortunate? Have we gone out of our way to visit the sick?

So many of us live in our own little cells and forget that our Savior made it His practice to help those who were distressed in body and soul. We work for our own advancement and are not troubled if our gain makes loss for another. Sometimes we actually scheme and plan how we may take advantage of our neighbors or those with whom we do business. Yet we profess to know God and to be His people.

How can this be? Jeremiah told King Jehoiakim that a man who knew God would be just in all his dealings and considerate of the poor and needy.

We say that we are Christians, that we know God. We profess to have received His Son as Savior. We claim His salvation. If profession is true, we will want to bear witness to the fact by living not just for ourselves but with every thought for those about us. We will pray for them and speak kindly to them. We will help them when they are in need. We will comfort them when they are in sorrow. We will be content with what we can earn in an honest way, a way that does not bring injury to others.

Let us remember Jehoiakim. Let not his ways be our ways.

22

Counterfeit Religion
JEREMIAH 23

I listened to him preach for several months. He talked about the wonder of the stars. He quoted poetry from time to time. I remember how on one occasion he showed utter unfamiliarity with the authors he quoted by his woeful mispronunciation of the name of a well-known German poet. What did he preach about? To this day I do not know. I doubt whether he himself did. His sermons were filled with empty phrases and vacuous expressions.

He was the pastor of a church in southern California. One day I asked him why he never preached on the great texts of the Bible that concern sin, salvation, eternal life and the atonement of the Lord Jesus Christ. He had forgotten his appointment with me and so, as I sat on the rim of the bathtub, he talked as he shaved in preparation for a Rotary Club dinner. However, he stopped long enough to say that one couldn't preach about everything and that the reason he didn't preach about the things I mentioned was that there were so many other subjects in the Bible to present—"one couldn't possibly preach on them all."

He was supposedly a minister of Jesus Christ, but I could come to only one conclusion: The "gospel" he preached was a counterfeit religion.

Counterfeit Religion at Work

The preacher I have described was little different from many of the prophets who prophesied in the time of Jeremiah, as one may discover by reading the 23rd chapter of Jeremiah's Book. Never commissioned by God to declare His Word, they had never received a call from God to represent Him. Yet they claimed divine authority for what they spoke. They tried to make people believe that they were true prophets of the Lord. To do so, it was necessary that they lie. They did!

Moreover, their message was a false one. They pronounced benediction and blessing on men who despised God. To those who sinned willfully, they said, "No harm will come to you" (Jer. 23:17). In other words, instead of pointing out and condemning sin, as they would have done if they had been true prophets, they made their living by quieting men's consciences and assuring the wicked that they need have no fear of judgment.

During the reign of King Zedekiah, one of these false prophets, Hananiah, boldly contradicted Jeremiah's prophecy of seventy years of captivity for the Jews in Babylon and declared that within two years Nebuchadnezzar's power over the Jews would be broken. By such a prophecy of encouragement to the rulers of Judah, he doubtless thought to court favor with Zedekiah. He didn't care that he lied before God. In the face of such blasphemy it was necessary that Jeremiah confront Hananiah with these words: "The Lord has not sent you, yet you have persuaded this nation to trust in lies" (Jer. 28:15).

I should not be surprised if some of Jeremiah's contemporaries were somewhat confused by the conflicting messages of those who claimed to be prophets of God. Jeremiah claimed to be a prophet; Hananiah claimed to be a prophet. One said one thing; the other's prophecy denied that of the first. Who was right?

We have somewhat the same situation today. In many so-called

"Christian" churches the ministers have little to say about sin, God's displeasure with it, or the need for a Savior from sin. Instead, a great deal is said about world peace, the universal fatherhood of God and brotherhood of man, racial relations, and similar topics. Labels have sometimes been given to such pastors—"Liberals," "Modernists," "Free-thinkers," et cetera, but most of them would prefer to be called just "Christian Ministers." They make no attempt to preach the whole counsel of God, but one of them once threw his Bible across the sanctuary, expressing himself to the effect that the Bible obscured God to the vision of men.

Counterfeit Religion Unmasked

While it is true that by God's common grace there may be many commendable things done by these ministers, at least from the point of view of simple humanitarianism, we must nevertheless consider the content of their message. Is it, in the final analysis, the heart of God's revelation, or is it a counterfeit religion? If the Scriptures are the Word of God, the religion of these men is false, for it omits the very heart of the gospel. It parades itself as bona-fide Christianity, but it is not. It is a masked deceiver. As Dr. J. Gresham Machen, that staunch defender of the faith, put it: There is an absolute antithesis between Christianity and the "gospel" such men preach. That "gospel" is a deadly foe of Christianity, and those who herald it are not ambassadors of Christ. They are false prophets. Their religion is a false one.

God is well aware of what is going on in our churches today. He knew what the false prophets were saying in Jeremiah's time. And he was acquainted with the lies that issued from the mouth of Hananiah. Did someone doubt His knowledge in this respect? His answer was unmistakable: "Can anyone hide in secret places so that I cannot see him?" (Jer. 23:24).

Conquering the Counterfeit

It would be well if, before deciding on what to preach, ministers would sit down and read certain passages in God's Word. Among these might be the teachings emphasized by the apostle Paul: the universality of sin; the penalty of sin, death; the need of justification;

Christ's vicarious sacrifice; the need of a new birth and of faith. These considered, would that they might read Paul's words: "But even if we or an angel from heaven should preach a gospel other than the one we preached to you, let him be eternally condemned" (Gal. 1:8). Would that they might turn to the first Book of the Bible and read: "You are the God who sees me" (Gen. 16:13). Could they then be bold enough to enter their pulpits and preach morality and brotherhood to the complete exclusion of the redemptive work of Christ?

Some seemingly dare to do so, but probably most offenders have been misled by others and are not conscious that theirs is a counterfeit religion. Regardless of their motivation, the all-seeing God has an all-powerful Word, and that Word is able to overthrow every false prophecy of man. God declares His Word to be like a consuming fire against all counterfeit religion. He says that His Word is "like a hammer that breaks a rock in pieces" (Jer. 23:29).

It is so. Hananiah's prophecy was never fulfilled. Those who believed it were sadly disillusioned and died in captivity in Babylon. Hananiah himself died, as God had said he would, in the seventh month of the same year.

A young Universalist minister once admitted that the congregations of most liberal churches—his own included—are not very faithful in their church attendance, while the members of many evangelical churches gather regularly in great numbers to hear God's truth. That admission amounted to a testimony that God's true revelation will untimately endure, while counterfeit religion falls into decay.

Let us therefore, not be misled by the subtle teachings of counterfeit religion, which come from man and not from God. Let us be as discerning and as fearless as Jeremiah. Let us "test the spirits to see whether they are from God" (1 John 4:1). Remember this: God is omnipresent and omniscient and knows the false prophets and their spurious prophecies. Let us be encouraged by this thought: The gospel that God has given us is like fire and like a mighty hammer. But while we condemn all counterfeit religion, unmask it and contend against it, let us also witness to the truth as it is in Jesus, our dear Redeemer and sovereign Lord.

23

The Lord Our Righteousness
JEREMIAH 23:5, 6

"The days are coming," declares the Lord,
  "when I will raise up to David a righteous Branch,
a King who will reign wisely
  and do what is just and right in the land.
In his days Judah will be saved
  and Israel will live in safety.
This is the name by which he will be called:
  The Lord Our Righteousness."

I wonder how many Christians are familiar with a certain Old Testament name given our Savior. It is this: "The Lord Our Righteousness." The prophet Isaiah once opened, as it were, a beautiful casket of precious jewels, divine names for our divine Redeemer. They strike us as being matchless names—Wonderful Counselor, Mighty God, Everlasting Father, Prince of Peace (Isa.

9:6). But are they more beautiful, more meaningful than the single gem of superb luster that another prophet holds before our eyes, "The Lord Our Righteousness"?

A Great Need

A sign on top of a building in one of our great American cities once proclaimed to the thousands of people who thronged the streets below this message: "Righteousness Exalteth a Nation: But Sin Is a Reproach to Any People."

It is a true statement. Men readily admit its veracity. Yet it is questionable whether the people of that city were any more righteous or felt any special need for righteousness because of the reminder that greeted them when they lifted their eyes and saw the words of our God written on the city's skyline.

That city today is in need of righteousness. What city is not? Our country is not exempt from the need for righteousness. And how sad a state our world at large lies in at present as far as morality is concerned!

Six hundred years before Christ the situation in Judah was little different. Perhaps it was worse. Even those who sat on the throne of the little Palestinian kingdom were immoral men. To oppression, violence and bloodshed, they added the sin of adultery.

Nothing could have been more contrary to the will of Judah's God as declared in the moral law of the Scriptures, nor could God wink at the gross sins of the rulers of His people. To be sure, the people themselves had in large measure yielded to the same sins, but the kings were doubly guilty in that they should have exerted all their power to lead their subjects into ways of righteousness.

The Promised Branch

Their failure to do so necessitated divine action. One after another of the prophets outlined the picture of what God would surely bring to pass. The line of Judah's kings was represented as a mighty tree with many branches. It had flourished for many years, but one day God would lay an axe to the tree. It would topple to the ground.

The roots, however, would not die, for they represented the rule of the man after God's own heart, the royal David, to whom God had sworn that from his seed should come one whose kingdom would endure forever. In God's own time there would come from that holy root a branch or shoot. At first it would appear mean and of no account, but in the end it would reach a state of sturdy growth, much power and great exaltation, and from it would come perfect and abundant fruit for the purifying and healing of the nations.

True believers understood these word pictures of the prophets as prophecies of their coming Messiah. Nor did they err in so doing, for the branch or shoot that would come forth out of the stump and roots of Jesse's son was described as righteous, the Savior of His people, the destroyer of wickedness, the builder of a spiritual temple, a majestic Priest-King. Only the promised Messiah could fit such a description.

The Efficacious Sacrifice

When the Messiah came, people did not refer to Him as the "Righteous Branch." They did not call Him by the title "The Lord Our Righteousness." He did not assume in a formal way the names from Isaiah's casket. But the meaning of these titles was drawn in living characters in His life, death, resurrection and ascension, and in the teachings of the apostles concerning His person and work.

The significance of the name "The Lord Our Righteousness" is perhaps not too clear to most of us. It means that through Him who bore it God would take away sin, crush the power of Satan, and flood the earth with righteousness as the waters cover the sea.

In referring to the righteous "Branch," Zechariah said that in one day He would remove iniquity from His people (Zech. 3:8, 9)—and how true were the prophet's words. One day on Golgotha the "Righteous Branch" became sin for us that "in him we might become the righteousness of God" (2 Cor. 5:21).

His sacrifice was efficacious in a twofold way: First, in that He died for us, we are legally righteous. The law has no longer any claim against us, because Christ has paid our debt and set us free. Secondly, in that our rebirth and sanctification are fruits of Calvary, His death on the cross was necessary if we were to become morally righteous.

When Jeremiah prophesied of The Lord Our Righteousness, it is quite probable that he was thinking only of Christ as the Author of moral righteousness among men, in contrast to the ungodly influence on the nation of the then-reigning kings of Judah. But when we think of Christ as The Lord Our Righteousness, we do well to put into the name the full New Testament content.

We, as His people, are clothed in His righteousness, without which we would be unworthy to come before God, but with which we may boldly come to the throne of grace and receive of His favor as though we had never sinned. But more! The Lord Our Righteousness has renewed in us, His people, His own holy image and purified our lives, even as it was prophesied that He would wash away "the filth of the women of Zion" (Isa. 4:4).

All righteousness comes from Him. The cross was a veritable fountain of righteousness, and from it has flowed and will flow, back into the past and on into the yet-unborn future, the only streams of righteousness that can wash away the guilty stains of our sin.

Thoughtfully, reverently, with deep emotion and true thankfulness, let us express to God our gratitude for His gift of The Lord Our Righteousness.

24

Chastised but Content
JEREMIAH 29:1-14

The trek of a conquered people into captivity is a pathetic sight. Tradesmen unaccustomed to physical exertion are herded along, weary and footsore and faint. Old men who have known better days are cursed by guards as they stumble on the march. Little children cling to their mothers' skirts and cry. Families become separated—forever.

Nor do the cruelties suffered or the heartaches endured end when the journey comes to a close. The strange land of adoption is seldom friendly. The newcomers are fortunate if they escape slavery. They are no longer a nation, no longer free. They long for the familiar scenes of the homeland. Their hearts are not at rest.

A portion of the populace of Jerusalem found themselves in this sad state in Babylon after the hostile armies of Nebuchadnezzar had invaded the temple city, raided the sanctuary, and made off with a select portion of the people, including the king and queen.

In the providence of God, the prophet Jeremiah was left behind in Jerusalem, but he did not forget the faithful souls among the covenant people who had been exiled to Nebuchadnezzar's capital city. He knew how discouragement would be apt to press upon them, and so one day he sent to them by the hand of Elasah and Gemariah a letter of comfort and instruction.

Chastisement Understood

Jeremiah was concerned that the exiles have a correct understanding of the catastrophe that had overtaken them. Were it due to blind fate, they might well despair. It was not. It was the work of their own covenant God. For those who still clung to the covenant that God had established with Israel long years before, the present captivity was not of the nature of righteous vengeance. It was merely *chastisement*. As so beautifully expressed in the twelfth chapter of Hebrews, chastisement comes only to sons. It is administered by a loving Father and is intended to be corrective rather than punitive. It is given that the fruit of righteousness may appear.

It was quite necessary that the captive Jews look on their exile in its true light. It was to be a testing and purifying period in their history. This was not their end as a people, but as a nation they had sunk to a state of ignominious sin and disregard for God's law. Something had to be done, or complete degradation would soon result. The corrective measure would have to be a severe one. So Jeremiah explained that Israel's own God had caused His people to be "carried into exile from Jerusalem to Babylon."

It is not true that all suffering is the direct result of sin. When our Lord healed the blind man spoken of in John 9, He declared that the man's blindness was due neither to his own sin nor to that of his parents, but "happened so that the work of God might be displayed in his life." However, we may go so far as to say that the design of all chastisement is to produce *righteousness*. The child of God may know that chastisement is of God. It is included in the "all things" in which "God works for the good of those who love him" (Rom. 8:28), "so that the man of God may be thoroughly equipped for every good work" (2 Tim. 3:17).

So often we err and go astray; we need to be taught obedience. So often we are proud; we need to learn to be humble. So often we depend on self; we need to be schooled in depending on God. Chastisement is the school in which we learn these lessons. The One who sends us to this school is God. The discouraged Israelites in Babylon needed to know this, and we may profit by a like knowledge.

Chastisement Borne

There are two possible responses to chastisement: *resignation* on the one hand, *rebellion* on the other. Open defiance of God's disciplinary measures makes for bitterness of soul and extreme unhappiness. Quiet submission to God's will brings peace and blessing. There are many who are strongly tempted to rebel, many who yield to that temptation.

In the hope that the Jewish captives would not rebel and find themselves fighting against God, Jeremiah counseled them to be content with their land of adoption. They should build homes and plant gardens and settle down to as happy a domestic life as possible. They should pray for the peace and prosperity of the government that now sheltered them. Its peace would be their peace.

Chastisement does not exclude blessing. It all depends on how we accept it. It is quite possible to endure much suffering of every kind and still have a heart that sings within us and blesses the name of Him who is the author of chastisement. The apostle to the Gentiles felt the rod of affliction as few others have ever done, but his prayer was ever that of his Lord, "May your will be done" (Matt. 26:42), and so he was able to say, "I have learned to be content whatever the circumstances" (Phil. 4:11).

Can we make that statement ours? As Christians, we should!

Chastisement Left Behind

Though chastisement, properly received, brings blessing, it is yet true that the scourged son experiences a constant longing for a better state. He looks forward to the time when chastisement will be a thing of the past. He can praise God in his state of affliction, but he awaits the time of deliverance.

The exiles in Babylon were to live in the present; they were also to live in the future, to lay hold on hope according to the wonderful promises of their God. In the dark days of the captivity they were not to forget the God who had wrought for them so many miracles of grace during the checkered history of their nation. In Babylon as in Jerusalem they could pray to their God. They could read and study the inspired writings, the Law and the prophets. They could still sing the songs of Zion. Though the temple sacrifices would no longer burn on the brazen altar, they could bring sacrifices of thanksgiving and obedience and purity of heart to the Lord.

Had some of them wandered from fellowship with God before they left their native land? Jeremiah urged them to re-establish that lost communion. They could again find the God of mercy and taste of His goodness, but they must seek Him with all their hearts. They must separate themselves from the sins they had loved and practiced. They must worship Him with singleness of heart and live to His glory.

If they would respond in this way and remain faithful, then there would be a sure reward. The day would come when they would leave chastisement behind and go out of captivity, back to the land they loved. So Jeremiah promised, and so God in His appointed time made it happen.

For the Christian who accepts chastisement as from God and submits humbly to the will and discipline of the heavenly Father, there is also a reward. For all such, Jesus has gone into heaven to prepare a place. Someday they will leave all chastisement behind and enter into that heavenly home.

While you tarry here as a stranger in the valley of chastisement, seek God with all your heart, content whatever happens, assured that God's discipline is for your own good. Make sure of your salvation. And look forward with confident expectation to that better land, where chastisement is no more!

25

The New Covenant

JEREMIAH 31:31-34

"The time is coming," declares the Lord,
"when I will make a new covenant
with the house of Israel
and with the house of Judah.
It will not be like the covenant
I made with their forefathers
when I took them by the hand
to lead them out of Egypt,
because they broke my covenant,
though I was a husband to them,"
declares the Lord.

"This is the covenant I will make with the house of Israel
after that time," declares the Lord.
"I will put my law in their minds
and write it on their hearts.
I will be their God,
and they will be my people.

No longer will a man teach his neighbor,
   or a man his brother, saying, 'Know the Lord,'
because they will all know me,
   from the least of them to the greatest,"
      declares the Lord.
"For I will forgive their wickedness
   and will remember their sins no more."

I t was in early December. A nationwide radio broadcast was coming to its close. An announcement promised that a calendar would be sent by the sponsors of the broadcast to each person sending in his name and address and requesting it. In the ensuing days thousands of listeners wrote in to accept the offer, and the calendars were mailed.

I have described for you a covenant. In the language of a catechism for little children, a covenant is defined as "an agreement between two or more persons." The broadcast sponsors had pledged themselves to a certain course of action. Certain of their listeners had agreed to the terms of the offer, namely, to send in their names and addresses. By so doing they had entered into an agreement and formed a covenant. It was therefore morally incumbent on those who had made the offer to keep the covenant and send the promised gifts.

A New Covenant Needed

The history of ancient Israel had witnessed the formation of a covenant before the smoking mountain of Sinai. It was a solemn covenant, for by it God condescended to make of a stiffnecked people a chosen and favored nation. By the terms of the covenant, God took Israel to be His people; they took the Lord Almighty to be their God. He promised to bless and protect them; they promised to obey His commands. An agreement was made. A covenant was established.

The covenant bound the children of Israel to the performance of many external ceremonies. They observed appointed feasts. They brought bullocks, goats and lambs to be placed as sacrifices on the great altar of the tabernacle. Human mediators, the priests, were the only ones allowed to enter the Holy Place. Once each year the high priest entered the Holy of Holies and sprinkled the blood of the sacrifice upon and before the mercy seat. Thus the common people were largely separated from God in worship.

But there was hope in and through the covenant: hope of forgiveness, hope of salvation! The moral law as written in the Ten Commandments convinced the people of their lack of righteousness and the absolute need for atonement and forgiveness. The sacrificial system emphasized the fact that there could be no forgiveness except through the shedding of blood, and by type and symbol prefigured a better sacrifice than that of bulls and goats.

As the years went by, some strove to keep the covenant; others forsook its obligations and chose the easier path of sin. God remained faithful, but the people broke the covenant. To the extent to which it was broken, it became of no effect. Its preservation depended on the obedience of a people who were by nature disobedient. When it was broken, the people were left under a terrible curse, even as the terms of the covenant had threatened. The mercy of heaven was shut off. The knowledge of God, which alone can purify and give peace, was withdrawn. The Israelites were left to the consequences of their sins.

With the covenant broken, the darkness of sin pressed ever more heavily on the land of Israel. Despite their reforms, the righteous kings of the nation had not been able to stem the tide of evil. The prophets warned in vain. The ominous threat of invasion loomed large on the horizon like a cloud of terrible destruction. Israel appeared doomed. O for a *new* covenant! O for a renewed compact with God! O for a covenant that would change hearts and make them love the law of the Lord! O for a covenant that could not be broken by man!

A New Covenant Promised

This was not the cry of an apostate people. It was the cry of the bleeding heart of a prophet who loved his country and his people. It was the cry of one who, with aching soul, had sought to bring those people back to God, only to see them go on in their sinful course, indifferent to his pleading and to the word of judgment that he brought them from God. This was the cry of Jeremiah.

Perhaps it was because the God of heaven heard the prophet's cry that He put the prophecy of a new covenant on the lips of this faithful servant. At any rate, a glorious announcement was made by the prophet:

> *"The time is coming," declares the Lord,*
>   *"when I will make a new covenant*
> *with the house of Israel*
>   *and with the house of Judah."*

He went on to say that it would be an everlasting covenant, not to be broken, not to be cast aside.

Look at your Bible. The first thirty-nine books are designated "The Books of the Old Testament." What does the word "Testament" mean? Cross it out and put in its place its equivalent, the word "Covenant." On the fly-leaf preceding the Gospel of Matthew make a similar change so that it reads not "The New Testament" but "The New Covenant." Now you can understand the promise made by God through Jeremiah.

The purpose of the two covenants was the same, that God would be the God of the covenant people and that they would belong to Him. The condition of the two covenants was the same, that His great lovingkindness and abundant grace would shelter them.

But though the old covenant was veiled in shadows and types, the new covenant would rest on a historical sacrifice: God's one and only Son shedding His blood to take away, once and for all, the sins of His elect or covenant people. Though the old covenant was written on tables of stone, the new covenant would be applied to the heart by the mighty working of the Spirit of God, the result being that the heart would be inclined toward God to ascertain His will and obey His law. Though the old covenant could be broken, the new covenant, by virtue of the abiding transformation wrought by the Holy Spirit, could never be broken!

Christian, have you ever meditated on the wonderful grace of God that made you a child of the covenant? Except for His grace, you would be without God and without hope in the world. But more! Christian, have you ever meditated on the wonderful grace of God that made you a child of the new covenant rather than the old? You had no choice in the matter. Can you do less than close your eyes and thank Him for the new covenant and His grace in bringing you into it?

26

Jeremiah's Book

JEREMIAH 36

*Take a few moments and read the chapter that
tells about "Jeremiah's Book."*

S ometimes the publication of a new book is eagerly awaited. But new books appear on the market every day, and most volumes would never be missed if they remained unpublished. We have so very many books—perhaps too many! It was not so in former days. We read of Lincoln and how the two or three books of his youth were precious beyond description. We think of the great library at Alexandria and how the destruction of its priceless store of books robbed us of the works of many ancient authors—works that have not been preserved elsewhere. But think of the uniqueness of a new book appearing six centuries before the birth of Christ!

The Book Dictated

When one day the manuscript of this new book was read in the city of Jerusalem, there was much interest and excitement. It was a book of sermons, messages that were intimately related to the political life and welfare of Judah. They had much to say about the future fate of the nation. Like the noble poetry of Milton, this book also was the product of dictation. A faithful scribe had penned with all accuracy the words that fell from the lips of a great preacher. The scribe was Baruch; the preacher was Jeremiah.

The value of this book lay neither in its selling power nor in the general scarcity of books. But the real author was not the preacher who dictated the book to Baruch. The real author was God. Large portions of the book purported to be the very words of God. The rest were set down by the authority of God. The book was God's message, not Jeremiah's. Had a dreamer or fanatic composed the work, it would have been valueless, but in it the very God of heaven spoke. For this reason, the man with a conscience trembled at the recitation of its contents.

The book was written for a purpose. Judah had long nursed a wicked heart. This caused her to depart from the worship of the true God. It led her to seek ungodly, immoral paramours, that is, to ally herself with heathen neighbors in both politics and religion. It constrained her people to violate God's commands with reckless abandon. Jeremiah's book was God's way of announcing judgment on the nation because of its awful sin. It was God's way of saying to a guilty people, "Turn! Turn from your evil ways! Why will you die?" (Ezek. 33:11). It was God's invitation to sinners to repent and receive forgiveness at the hand of the righteous Sovereign of heaven and earth.

The Book Destroyed

The one man who most needed to hear the message of this book was Judah's king, Jehoiakim. He had led the people into sin; it was for him to lead them to repentance. He was the leader; others were but followers. His throne and kingdom were threatened with doom; it was his duty to seek clemency and so to save the condemned state. Therefore, God saw to it that Jeremiah's book was placed in his hands without delay.

How was it received? With respect? With tears? With godly sorrow? With reverent fear? Had Pharaoh a hardened heart, Jehoiakim's was no less unbending. Confirmed sinner that he was, he gave no thought to repentance, but with carefully calculated wickedness he seized the scroll of prophecy, plunged his penknife recklessly through it, and cast it into the fire on the hearth. Greedy tongues of flame hasted to lick its edges, gathered themselves together, and sent up a flare that momentarily lighted the dark corners of the winter-house. Seconds later, only curled leaves of ash remained.

Perhaps this was the first time a portion of the Scriptures was deliberately destroyed, yet it was not the last. The Bible bonfires of infidels and even church authorities have lighted the centuries of the Christian era. God's Book, which condemns sin and offers the free gift of a Savior from sin, has suffered much at the hand of sinners. Voltaire thought to destroy it from the face of the earth and in so doing to bring to an end the sect of Christians. England's skies once burned red from incendiary piles fed by the leaves of God's Book. In this way, people despised God's offer of mercy, rebelled at the accusation of sin, and committed sacrilege against the volume in which is found the way of forgiveness and life everlasting.

The Book Rewritten

If King Jehoiakim thought that God's Word could be so easily destroyed once and for all, he was badly mistaken. Neither the human author nor the faithful scribe was allowed to fall into his hands. As they had once yielded themselves to be instruments of God, so they performed the same service again. The lips that had dictated the scroll burned by the king spoke again the same words and added more. The hand that had guided the pen across the original scroll was faithful in a like task. The book of the prophet was rewritten and enlarged.

Jehoiakim died, as Jeremiah said he would. Unrepentant Judah went into captivity, as Jeremiah had prophesied. Seventy years elapsed, and a faithful remnant returned to the Jewish homeland, as Jeremiah had promised. In the fullness of time, the Righteous Branch came from the root of Jesse, even as Jeremiah had described. The new covenant announced by the prophet was written on the hearts of God's people.

What was the fate of the inspired Book during this time? Were the prophecies fulfilled while the Book itself perished? Not so! Greek translations of the Book became somewhat distorted, but the true text in the original Hebrew tongue was preserved in remarkable fashion. Is it not written, "Heaven and earth will pass away, but my words will never pass away" (Matt. 24:35)? Other books have been lost in the dust of the ages; Jeremiah's Book was not lost, for it was God's Book, a very real part of the Book of Books, and the providential care of God kept it safe through the years.

In the year 1800 in Manchester, England, a man guilty of burning the Bible lay on his deathbed, refusing to hear the Scriptures read, refusing to pray. His plight was terrible indeed and was mirrored in the hopeless confession he uttered as well as in the curses that poured from his mouth. I have no fear that any of us will go out and burn the Bible. I do not think we would be guilty of boasting ability to rid the world of the Bible as did Voltaire. But I am just a little afraid that perhaps some of us, or others like us, will, as did King Jehoiakim, pay little heed to what God's Book has to say about sin and the need for repentance.

One does not have to burn the Bible to come into condemnation, though doing so would add to his or her guilt. All one has to do is to be indifferent to the warning and invitation of the Word, and that is such an easy thing to do! God's Book says that we have sinned. The Bible says that the unrepentant sinner will go away into everlasting punishment. It says that "God so loved the world that he gave his one and only Son, that whoever believes in him shall not perish but have eternal life" (John 3:16). Yes, it urges upon all the necessity of trusting in Christ as Savior and Lord. One who does not turn from sin to Christ might just as well burn the Book that offers pardon and life.

Let no one commit such great folly! Instead, let one and all turn and believe and receive, for salvation is the free gift of God.

27

The Sin of Vacillation
JEREMIAH 37:11–38:28

An analogy used by the translators of the King James Version has found its place in the English language; *unstable as water*. Now instability and vacillation are sisters. What is true of the one is true of the other, and water is about the most unstable substance imaginable. I drop the anchor of my boat. It falls like a plummet to the bottom, dividing the waters like a knife. But as speedily as the waters separate, just so quickly do they reunite. I lay my hand gently on the water's surface. Under its simple weight the waters flee away, only to return when the hand is removed. I take a tiny feather that the wind has tossed about with abandon. It is a poor instrument, but even so it is powerful enough to cut the water's surface and disturb the glass-like calm. Who would like a moral character as changeable, as unstable as water? A vacillating person has such a character.

Vacillation Defined

Vacillation is commonly considered a sign of weakness. We know what is right but we do not have the courage and strength of moral character to follow the right. Usually we are willing to disobey conscience and sin against God. Still we consider the right way, which is generally the hard way. We are somewhat inclined to go that way because it is the honorable way and the way of truth. Yet we fear the consequences. We are afraid of what people will say about us and do to us. As we see our lives or positions or health in jeopardy, we quickly gravitate toward another course. In the end, we take the easy way and endeavor to appease conscience by all manner of excuses. That is vacillation—and sin!

Vacillation is bad enough in any circumstance. But it is most serious and deplorable when one is confronted directly by the Word of God. God lays on us specific commands. We admit His sovereignty and the rightness of what He tells us to do. Without question and without delay, we ought to obey. The unstable person does not. Prone to indecision, he thinks it over. Half resolved to obey, he hesitates. The price of obedience is too high. Selfish desires would have to be sacrificed. He dwells on those desires and the prospect of fleshly delights that they will bring. Then, having entered into temptation, he yields.

It is so also with the invitations and promises of God. God urges sinners to confess their inability to save themselves, to trust in Christ for salvation, and to come humbly to Him for eternal life. The vacillating person believes and trembles but is true to his nature and never takes the final step of casting from him the crutches of his own righteousness and grasping the cross of Christ as his only hope.

Vacillation Illustrated

As I read Jeremiah 37 and 38, I am particularly struck by the vacillation of King Zedekiah. Zedekiah had come to the throne in troubled times. It was Nebuchadnezzar who had appointed him ruler in Jerusalem, and he ruled only at the pleasure of that monarch.

For several years Zedekiah tolerated the arrangement, but finally he rebelled against the overlordship of Babylon. It was a disastrous move. In the ninth year of Zedekiah's reign, Nebuchadnezzar and the Babylonian army came with the set purpose of taking the city and putting down the rebellion. They took up the siege of the city, and soon famine threatened the inhabitants. The situation was grave.

At this juncture, the king remembered the prophet Jeremiah, who shortly before, on a false pretext, had been thrown into a dungeon. Zedekiah knew that the only real hope for the deliverance of the city lay in the God whom Jeremiah served. He recalled how God had freed Jerusalem from a like siege by the Assyrian army in the time of King Hezekiah. Perhaps God would deliver the city again. He would ask the prophet.

In accordance with his decision, he removed Jeremiah from the dungeon and talked with him in secret, only to learn that God would have the defending forces capitulate to the Chaldeans and seek mercy at their hands. Zedekiah would not consent to such a course of action. It was entirely distasteful to him. Moreover, he feared the wrath of the princes if it should become known that he was even considering such a move.

The rest of the story is but a rehearsal of how he sought to protect Jeremiah from ill at the hands of the princes, only to deliver him over to them when they sought his life. These princes hated the prophet, his prophecy of doom for the nation, and his insistence that the only thing to do was to surrender; and though Zedekiah would have shown him a certain amount of favor as God's prophet, yet he dared not run the risk of incurring their enmity.

Weighed in God's balance, Zedekiah was found wanting. But what was his sin? It lay not alone in deliberate rebellion against God and divine ordinances. Zedekiah's sin was not so much in the form of wickedness and defiance of God as was that of Jehoiakim. One gains from the Bible record the impression that Zedekiah was at times inclined to listen to God's prophet and do what was right. He was prevented from doing so by his own weakness and vacillation.

Vacillation Condemned

In summarizing Zedekiah's life, the Scriptures read like this: "He did evil in the eyes of the Lord" (2 Kings 24:19). That is God's way of saying that vacillation is a grievous sin and itself worthy of condemnation.

Also in God's Word we are told that this man, who was too lacking in moral character to do the revealed will of God, fled from Jerusalem when it fell after a two-year siege, was captured in flight, and was severely punished by his captors. His sons and Judah's princes were executed in his presence, after which his own eyes were put out, and he was carried away to die in captivity. God did not save him from this catastrophe. Again, that was God's way of saying that vacillation is a sin that removes one from divine protection, love and mercy.

Fortunately, there is a cure for this dread disease. Our Lord says to us, "My power is made perfect in weakness" (2 Cor. 12:9). Paul declared, "I can do everything through him who gives me strength" (Phil. 4:13). God could have strengthened Zedekiah and made him steadfast in moral character, but Zedekiah refused to commit his life to God. He who trusts in Christ as his Savior, though he is by nature vacillating, can and should have a moral character firm and unmoveable, for Christ is then the Rock on whom he rests.

The first thing we must do is to make sure that Christ is our Rock. The second is to trust Him to supply strength of character in order that we may not waver in the moral walk of life set before us. Trusting in Christ for strength, let us make a threefold vow: To have nothing to do with evil, to be true to the Faith, and to do the right. This was once the Baptismal Vow of a certain church, but we may well appropriate it for ourselves. We must not vacillate in things moral or spiritual. In these spheres, vacillation is sin!

28

Insincere Promises

JEREMIAH 42:1–43:7

No twentieth century figure was more contemptible than Adolf Hitler. He was little worthy of respect. His pledged word could not be trusted. He promised one thing and did another. At a critical juncture he assured the world that a certain movement of territorial expansion was the last he and his country would seek. Not long afterward, the nations of the world awoke to the realization that his promise had been completely insincere. It had been given only to aid him in achieving his own desired ends. He may well go down in history as the Prince of Liars.

Stoutly Affirmed

That Adolf Hitler was not the first giver of insincere promises is attested by the history of the Jews after Nebuchadnezzar of Babylon had put an end to the rule of the line of David and left Gedaliah as governor in Jerusalem.

It was a time of confusion, conflict and bloodshed. Gedaliah was murdered. The assassin found his own position insecure and fled in the face of popular opposition. New leaders were recognized by the people, men proud in their own conceit.

For some reason—perhaps because they hoped for some favorable word from the prophet that would strengthen their hold over the people—they sought out Jeremiah, urged him to pray for them to the Lord, and stoutly affirmed that they would walk in whatever way God should direct.

Admitting the folly of their nation in disregarding God's prophetic warnings, they were emphatic in asserting that they had learned their lesson and would from that time on obey God in all things. It sounded as though they meant it. Jeremiah evidently thought so. Although it seemed too good to be true, it actually appeared as though they were sincere in their vows and had a heart desire to follow the ways of their covenant God.

How Jeremiah must have rejoiced! How many a pastor rejoices when some wayward soul unexpectedly confesses his wrong and declares that he is a changed person. Such instances are of common occurrence. A storekeeper with a guilty conscience rises in church, makes a confession of sin, and promises to live a new life. A man who has been untrue to his wife assures the minister that he will mend his ways. Someone known for spiritual indifference wants to join the church, puts on a garb of piety, makes a bold Christian profession, and is received into church membership. Surely, we feel, there must be rejoicing in heaven!

Severely Tested

Whether or not the people of Judah and their new leaders were in earnest in making a vow of obedience to God was shortly to be determined. The Babylonians had despoiled both the nation and its substance. Egypt was friendly, since it, too, was an object of conquest for Nebuchadnezzar. If there was a haven of rest for the harassed Jews, it seemed to be Egypt. In Egypt one might hope for safety, comfort and material abundance. Moreover, the band of Jews that had so staunchly affirmed their intention to follow

God's instructions had their minds made up to flee down into this land of refuge.

But God had constantly warned Judah against courting the friendship and help of the pagan people who lived in the land of the Nile. He had not changed one iota in that respect. Would the Jews obey God? Then let them stay out of this godless land! That was the word God had for Jeremiah to give to the people.

Like the words of God's Son in later times, it seemed like a "hard teaching." It ran directly contrary to any hope they may have had. The testing came at the sorest spot possible. If they really meant business, this test would tell.

God has a way of searching our motives and sincerity by testing us in like manner. The storekeeper is tested in regard to his particular sin, the unfaithful husband in regard to his, the once-indifferent man aspiring to church membership in regard to his. God is not satisfied with a general outward appearance of reformation. He confronts us directly with our past besetting sin and bids us choose between it and himself. Only such a testing will definitely establish our sincerity.

Contemptuously Broken

The dissembling of the Jews was immediately apparent. They had no intention whatever of altering their plans so that they would coincide with the revealed will of God. If God's directions had not crossed their own purposes, they undoubtedly would have advertised widely that they were nobly carrying out His desire. But when the prophetic word proved contrary to their design, they built higher the bars of deceit and claimed that Jeremiah was falsely representing God's word. By so doing, they revealed their contempt for promises made before the sovereign God.

Their actions offered swift and convincing proof of their insincerity. Taking Jeremiah and others with them, they hastened down into Egypt in direct disobedience to God's command. Promises to the contrary? Who could be simple enough to believe that they really meant them?

The storekeeper doubtless had a similar thought when he drifted back into a dishonest life, though I am sure he was not quite so insincere when he made his vows. The inconstant husband probably smiled to himself at the naïveté of the minister as he continued his life of infidelity. The new church member soon lost his cloak of piety, but was ever arrogant and unashamed. Their promises were insincere. They were contemptuously broken!

Did you ever, before God, take a vow concerning spiritual things? Have you kept that vow? Has it withstood severe testing and remained unbroken? Or did it amount only to so many words and little more?

It need not have been a promise made before men. Perhaps it was on a sickbed, and you told God you would serve Him and live for His glory if you were healed. Were you uttering mere words, words you have made no serious attempt to fulfill?

God hates all insincerity, all deceit. His moral law reads, "You shall not give false testimony" (Ex. 20:16). That concerns what you have to say about your neighbor; it also condemns *any* false pronouncement that you frame in your heart or let fall from your lips. You may deceive others by pretense of piety and earnestness, but not God.

It is good to repent of sin and pledge yourself, with Christ's help, to a new life of obedience to Him who is Lord of heaven and earth. It is an abominable thing, a thing severely condemned by God, to make false vows of any kind in the hope of achieving some kind of gain. It were far better if such insincere promises had never been made!

Stand in awe of God. He is a God of honesty and truth. Let your speech be straightforward and devoid of even the suggestion of deceit. You cannot deceive God, but you can reap His wrath!

29

Guilty Moab
JEREMIAH 48:7

As the traveler to the Holy Land stands on the western shore of the Dead Sea and gazes across the water, he is looking into the native land of Ruth the Moabitess. It appears as though this land is one of mountains that drop precipitously to the shores of the sea, but when one visits this ancient land, he finds it a high tableland, deeply carved by two rivers, the Arnon and the Zered. Like the Jews, the people who lived here in olden times were Semites. Their language and customs were much the same as those of Israel, but they had turned away from the worship of the God of Lot, from whom they were descended, and had gone away into idolatry and sin, worshiping Chemosh as their national god. Ruth, however, was ready to abandon these practices. In cleaving to Naomi her mother-in-law and forsaking the land of her birth, she was led to say, "Your people will be my people, and your God my God" (Ruth 1:16).

Moab's Cardinal Sin

This was what all the Moabites should have said, and they should have turned to the worship and righteousness of this God, whom Ruth was now to serve. But instead of trusting the Lord, they depended on their own abilities and resources.

God was not ignorant of their course, nor did He leave them undisturbed in their complacency and pride. Isaiah had lashed out against these cardinal sins of Moab. Amos had warned of God's judgments against her. It was left for Jeremiah to seal the prophetic testimony against this self-sufficient people, and Jeremiah did just that. Lifting up his voice against the sinful nation, he cried,

> *Since you trust in your deeds and riches,*
> *you too will be taken captive,*
> *and Chemosh will go into exile*
> *together with his priests and officials.*

Moab was guilty before God in that she trusted in what she could do. Were her borders attacked, she looked to her army for security. Would she overthrow the yoke of Ahab, mighty men were at her command. Did the bribery of Balaam fail, carrying out his further hellish schemes gave promise of success. Should the cisterns of her people go dry, they would build better ones. Whatever their undertaking, they relied on it to succeed. If it failed, they turned to some other expedient. They had no thought of calling on God to help them.

Chemosh, God of Accomplishment

But what of the nation's own deity, Chemosh? Did not the people trust in him? On the Moabite Stone, which bears an inscription by Mesha, king of Moab, this ruler says that Moab was oppressed many days "for Chemosh was angry with his land." Mesha attributes the deliverance of his nation to Chemosh. He tells of slaying the people of a city to please Chemosh. He declares that he set forth to war to do the bidding of Chemosh and that Chemosh gave him success. Surely it sounds as though Moab trusted in Chemosh, its god.

Moreover, in the case of King Mesha there is other evidence that he trusted, at least to some extent, in the god Chemosh. The Bible tells us that when the Moabites were in serious straits because of an attack by Israel that Mesha offered his son as a human sacrifice on the city wall, presumably to appease the wrath of Chemosh and so to turn the tide of battle (2 Kings 3:27). Such an act would require definite faith in the god and his power.

What then shall we say? Did Moab divide her trust between her own accomplishments and Chemosh her god? Precisely no, and for this reason: Chemosh was known for what he was supposed to have done. The God of Israel was a God of power and deliverance, but He was also concerned with faith, righteousness, spiritual life, salvation. Chemosh was not so. Chemosh was concerned only with Moabite achievement. Israel's Sovereign was a true and living God who had revealed Himself to men. Chemosh, like every other false god, was a god of the imagination, built up by men's fancies to symbolize and typify their chief interests and coincide in character with their special desires. It is for this reason that the gods of the nations were in character nothing like Israel's self-revealed God.

Gods Like Chemosh

Trust in a god like Chemosh and trust in one's own accomplishments go hand in hand. Not many modern scientists are professing atheists. Nearly everyone has his god, a god of achievement, a god like Chemosh. These gods are not the true God of the Bible, despite the general rejoicing in certain religious circles that science is now in harmony with Christianity. No, they are gods fashioned to fit the ideals of men interested primarily in the achievements of man. There is no pretense that these gods come from the Bible; they come from the laboratory. If they rise above laboratory conceptions, it is only because the laboratory god fails to meet the needs of man's soul, and the imagination is pressed to enlarge the notion of god so that it will.

After all, there really is little difference whether one trusts merely in deeds or in a god who professes to accomplish things. In a speech to the German nation, Adolf Hitler told his people that God would not help them unless they themselves took the initiative. Hitler had no respect for God. For him, God was like Chemosh, only a god of accomplishment. Is not godless Russia just as bad? She openly trusts in her abilities and accomplishments to the exclusion of any god whatsoever. The two are of one cloth, and both, like Moab, stand guilty before God.

We turn from nations to individuals. It is easy to see the guilt and condemn Hitler's Germany, modern Russia, and ancient Moab, but are our skirts clean? Have we not come somewhat under the impress of the spirit of the age in which we live, an age that more and more trusts in human achievement and makes that its god? It would be truly remarkable if we had not.

There is a real tendency to make our God such a god, to treat Him only as one who grants requests addressed to Him, opens doors, heals the flesh, and gives success to our undertakings. We do not treat Him as an eternal Spirit, to be worshiped in spirit and in truth. We do not give Him our hearts. We do not really love Him. We call Him by a different name, but is He only a "Chemosh" to us?

Think about the person who makes God that kind of a god. He, like Moab, actually trusts in what he does. He, like guilty Moab, is under the condemnation of God.

O that everyone burdened with such guilt might turn to the fountain where all guilt may be washed away, the fountain of Jesus' precious blood, which flowed from Calvary's cross. O that self-centered men and women might forsake trust in their own abilities, plunging a dagger into their pride and slaying it once for all. O that they might come to Christ and seek His pardon, trusting in Him and not in their own achievements. What a terrible thing on Judgment Day for one to have his name included with that of Moab and this sentence read: "Guilty! He trusted in his own accomplishments!"

30

Insecure Defenses
JEREMIAH 49:16

A lthough we are not presently at war, our nation has a defense department, a secretary of defense, an enormous defense budget. We are governed by a psychology of fear—fear that a war will break out suddenly and find us unprepared.

There was a time when most of us thought that the broad expanses of ocean on either side of our country would render it free from the danger of foreign invasion. We looked to the great natural barriers of water for our defense. Now all is different. We are in the nuclear age, and if an aggressor should direct nuclear weapons against us, we want to have adequate defenses. We therefore spend billions annually to protect our country in case there should be an attack. Our aim is to entrench ourselves so firmly that no power, however great, will be able to destroy us.

A Natural Fortress

Many years ago another nation viewed its natural defenses with satisfaction. That nation was Edom, a country southeast of the Dead Sea, a land peopled by the descendants of Esau. A rugged, mountainous country, it is strangely carved by the waters of nature, and abounding in high, almost inaccessible peaks.

Its capital city lies in a mountain-rimmed hollow. All about it tower rock cliffs, dull crimson in color with sprinklings of purple here and there. There are few approaches to the city. They proceed through narrow passes and along hazardous trails. The most important one follows along a deep and narrow defile, with massive rock walls hemming it in on either side and rising perpendicularly until their proud crowns stand high in the heavens. Here a handful of warriors might stand and defy an army.

Into the red cliffs of Edom its first inhabitants cut their dwellings and became known as cave dwellers. Here later peoples took up their abode and went on to carve rose-colored temples and spacious theaters into the sides of the walls of stone. They feared no enemy, for at God's hand they had received a home that manifestly needed little of man-made defenses to render it secure.

A Fortress of Pride

The people of Edom might conceivably have looked on their rock-bound home as that which indeed it was, a gift of God. They might have praised Him for the security they enjoyed. Humble before Creation's Maker, they might have trusted not in the rocks of nature but in the eternal God, the Rock of Ages.

They chose to do otherwise. Confident that their defenses were secure, they made no effort to seek the favor of God and taste of His grace. Feeling no need of His help, they had no love for His chosen people, who were their neighbors. When Israel needed help, Edom not only refused to come to her aid but improved the opportunity to step in and gain some spoil at her expense.

The Edomites became a self-satisfied people. Pride ruled their hearts. Though they had a name for wisdom, they employed terror rather than wisdom in dealing with others. With never a fear of the judgment of God, Edom went her own way and trusted in her own strength and the protecting peaks that reared their heads above her home.

A Fortress of Destruction

High on the jagged crags and overhanging ledges where nature forbids man to climb, the mighty eagle makes its nest. There is no interference. His solitary haunts are freshened by the soft moisture of the clouds and bathed in the pure sunlight of heaven.

No enemy can scale the dizzy heights and threaten the safety of the eagle young. Did the eagle dwell in Edom's mounts? If so, he looked down far below where the homes of humans dotted the sandstone cliffs. He could glide on his pinions down through the air to their dwelling places, but they could not reach the heights where he lived. Yet this is God's word to the proud people of Edom:

> *Though you build your nest as high as the eagle's,*
> *from there I will bring you down (Jer. 49:16).*

No eminence was towering enough to be beyond the reach of God's wrath. God looks down on the eagle, and God looks down on men, no matter how lofty their fortresses. The rock-walled chasms, forbidding defiles and narrow passes of Edom might succeed in turning away the thrusts of hostile armies, but they were insecure defenses as far as God was concerned. And because the Edomites were proud sinners, God's judgment would be visited on them despite every natural barrier or any other defense they might employ. "I will bring you down" meant destruction. Edom's mountains had deceived her. They had given her a sense of security, but it was a false one!

As individuals we evaluate our status in life. Our heritage has been a happy one. We have comfortable incomes, live in attractive homes, drive our automobiles, enjoy good health, receive the benefits of a good education and press buttons and switches to make electricity serve us. What more do we need? What have we to fear? Is not our happiness secure in these things?

Too often we in America think so. Like the Edomites, we live in supposedly impregnable fortresses, making little or no place in our lives for God. We feel secure without Him, and we do not pray:

> Rock of Ages, cleft for me,
> Let me hide myself in Thee.

We proudly spurn God's offer of salvation through Christ and His atoning work on the cross.

Some day we will find God's Word true: *"Though you* build your nest as high as the eagle's, from there I will bring you down." It will become evident that the things which have given us a feeling of security are fully as misleading as the rugged mountain defenses of Edom. God's judgment will bring us down from our lofty pride to a bitter end.

If we ignore the Lord Jesus Christ and trust in self, we can have no other hope. But may it not be so for one of us! May we, rather, commit ourselves to Christ, submit to the gracious rule of the Holy Spirit, and come to know the everlasting God as the Rock of our salvation. Then the fortresses of earthly pride will cease to attract us, and we will sing with Martin Luther:

> A mighty fortress is our God,
> A bulwark never failing . . .
> Dost ask who that may be?
> Christ Jesus, it is He;
> Lord Sabaoth His name,
> From age to age the same,
> And He must win the battle.

31

The Lost Sheep of Israel
JEREMIAH 50:4-7, 17-20

More picturesque words never fell from the lips of Jesus than those He addressed to a Canaanite woman; "I was sent only to the lost sheep of Israel" (Matt. 15:24). The flock was scattered, and the sheep were lost. But He was the Good Shepherd, come to seek and save the lost. And while His special mission was to the wanderers of Israel, it developed as the conversation continued that others astray on the mountains might also hear His loving voice, be taken up in His arms, nestle in His bosom, and be carried like lambs to the fold.

Astray

Long years before the Savior's coming, false shepherds let down the bars of the fold, and the sheep of Israel, with ears deaf to the voice of the true Shepherd, willfully left it to go with the false shepherds out on the mountains. From hill to hill they went. Abundant pasture and freedom from restraint caused them to forget their home. Then came times of danger. Wild beasts of the forest sought to destroy them, but their new shepherds offered them no protection. They found themselves helpless and lost. Such was the picture of Israel as drawn by Israel's Lord and made known to her by the prophet Jeremiah. At the time she found herself suffering blows of destruction from foreign conquerors and facing long and bitter captivity in Babylon.

The false shepherds were leaders who had seduced Israel away from the true God, the God whom their fathers had worshiped. The mountains where they had wandered were the high places. There the people went to worship idol gods. The lions that had set upon them in their helplessness were the kings of Assyria and Babylon. Truly the people who had once been sheltered by the protecting care of a God of love and grace were now as lost sheep, a flock on the verge of perishing.

It is a terrible thing to be lost! On one occasion, as the first heralds of winter had begun to strip the gorgeous foliage from the trees of the White Mountains, a little girl became separated from her parents and wandered for days in the desolate woods. She was like a straying lamb. Her only protection from the cold was the covering of leaves she placed over her body at night. Fortunately, no wild animals attacked her. Thousands spent those days in suspense, for all familiar with that mountain country knew only too well that if the child still lived she was probably on the verge of perishing.

If our concern is so great for a lost child, ought it not to be far greater for lost souls? Think of the millions who today follow teachers of false religions. Multitudes are misled by the false shepherds who pastor many of our churches. Think of the countless numbers who have wandered far away from God and are entirely indifferent to the things of the Spirit.

If one's life is lived apart from the Lord Jesus Christ, that person is a lost sheep. There is only one way to the fold of heaven. Jesus said, "I am the way." Is there good in non-Christian religions? Not enough to save one who is lost, without God and without hope! Will a good moral life save one from the wages of sin, which is spiritual death and everlasting separation from God? No, such a one is lost,

astray, and the Man of the Cross is his or her only hope. And is it
not a terrible thing to be astray from God?

Returning

The lost sheep of Israel found it so. Their condition was a miserable one. The idol gods they had served in place of the Lord Almighty
had proved to be a mockery. The proud citadel of Jerusalem in
which they had felt so secure had fallen to the enemy. Its inhabitants had become the prey of a people who, in destroying and
oppressing them, disclaimed guilt, saying,

> *We are not guilty,*
> *for they sinned against the Lord, their true pasture,*
> *the Lord, the hope of their fathers (v. 7).*

How stinging must have been the force of those words! Though it
was untrue that those who spoke them were clear of responsibility
and guilt before God, it was very true that Israel's pathetic state had
been brought on because of her own sin and departure from the
Lord God. With shame and remorse, the pitiable exiles had to admit
that it was so. As Daniel prayed in Babylon, his lips bore this
confession: All that had happened to Israel was but the just
punishment for her sin and apostasy.

As in the case of the prodigal son, there came a time when som
of the lost sheep of Israel thought again of the fold from which the
had wandered and of the Good Shepherd, whom they had forsaken.
They remembered the words of the prophets, that a remnant would
be saved. By the waters of Babylon they experienced godly sorrow
for their sins and vowed that they would seek the Lord, undertake
the long journey back to the homeland, and enter again into covenant with the all-gracious God. Jeremiah prophesied that it would
be so, and his prophecy was fulfilled.

Forgiven

The purpose of these lost sheep was good, but what of the Shepherd of the fold? Would He receive them again after they had
sinned against Him, ignored His commands, scorned His love and

guidance, and gone away after other gods? No charge of injustice could rightly be made against Him if He chose not to do so. With all tenderness and longsuffering He had sought to keep them from apostasy, to reclaim them before terrible judgment would fall upon the nation. Knowingly, stubbornly, they had refused His overtures of grace.

Yet His lovingkindness and plenteous mercy, as promised by Jeremiah, did not fail, nor was it turned away from the penitent exiles. Abundant pardon awaited those who had resolved to return to their God. But probably the full extent of His grace was unrecognized. It was this same God who had kept them from death in the land of captivity. It was He who had enabled them to make the homeward journey. It was He who waited with outstretched arms to pronounce them forgiven. It was God who had taken the initiative all along the way. Hear His words:

> *I will bring Israel back to his own pasture . . .*
> *I will forgive the remnant I spare.*

The truth is that salvation is of the Lord. He it is who saves, and He alone. His Word convicts us of sin. His Spirit gives us new life in Christ. His Son died in the place of sinners that they might be saved and all their iniquities forgiven—not only for the lost sheep of Israel but also for the lost of all races and places and ages who would put their trust in Him.

He has taken the initiative. The divine Son has borne the guilt. God wants those who are but lost sheep to seek Him and the heavenly Zion. If you are one of the lost sheep, perhaps He is even now moving your heart with the call to join yourself to Him in a perpetual covenant of salvation. Do not refuse His wooing, but accept the invitation to come to Him while it is yet the day of grace. Remember that many of the lost sheep of Israel perished away from the fold and were eternally lost. "Now is the time of God's favor, now is the day of salvation" (2 Cor. 6:2). Lost sheep of every nation, kindred, tribe and tongue are now invited to seek the Lord and be saved for time and eternity.